What can I do today?

Colour illustrations by Brian Edwards
Projects designed by Linda Nichol and David Clark (Design Group) Ltd

PURNELL
London

How to Enlarge Instruction Diagrams

Occasionally, in the instructions, you will find a diagram printed on a grid, this is to help you draw the required shape to the correct size. The following notes explain how to use the grid.

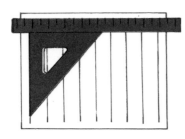

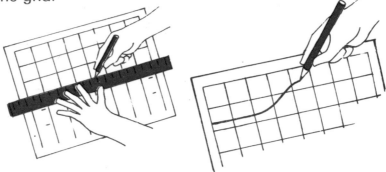

inches	millime
$\frac{1}{4} =$	
$\frac{1}{2} =$	1
$\frac{3}{4} =$	1
1 =	2
2 =	5
3 =	7
4 =	10
5 =	12
6 =	15
7 =	17
8 =	20
9 =	22
10 =	25
11 =	27
12 =	30
18 =	45
24 =	61
30 =	76
36 =	91
42 =	106
48 =	121
54 =	137
60 =	152

1. On the printed grid you will see the size of one square marked by arrows. This is the size each square must be when you draw your grid.

2. First mark out the correct number of upright lines near the top of your paper or card and then do the same near the bottom.

3. Pencil in the upright lines using a ruler to keep them straight.

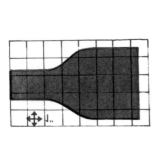

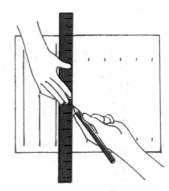

4. Use a set square to draw the top line of your grid. Place the ruler against it if it is not big enough.

5. Measure out the correct number of horizontal lines starting with the one you have just drawn, then pencil them in.

6. Now draw the shape onto your grid square by square. As an example, go back to drawing No. 1. You will see that the outline starts on the second square down. It goes horizontally across two squares, begins to go up on the third square, then goes right up into the top line at the fourth square and so on.

A number of projects included in this book have been previously published as Spears Project Cards.

Published in 1973 by Purnell
Printed and bound in Holland
© Stallergreen Ltd. 1973

SBN 361 02472 X

Contents

Care should be taken and guidance given to young children when using certain tools necessary for some projects in this book.

TOYS

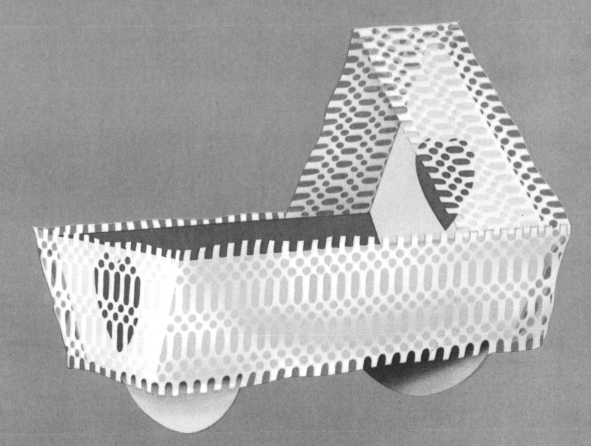

Dog

You will need:
Three squares of stiff paper
6″ × 6″

Cotton wool
Glue

Dog

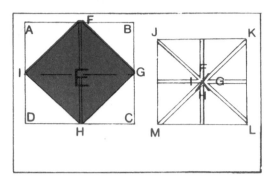

1. Fold points ABCD to point E. Turn over and fold points FGHI into centre as shown.

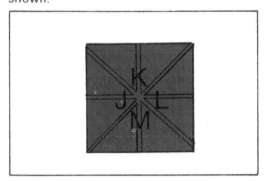

2. Turn over and fold points JKLM into centre as shown.

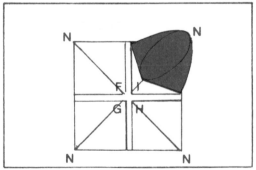

3. Turn over again and open out lines IN/HN/GN/FN as shown.

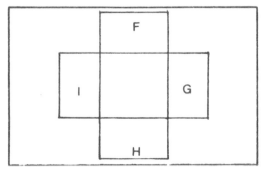

4. Now flatten out as diagram.

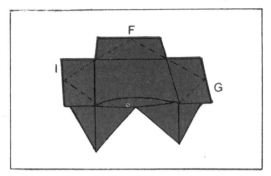

5. Fold points JKLM down as shown to make legs.

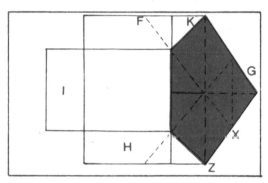

6. Now pull one side (G) out as shown and the opposite side (I).

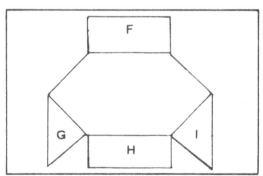

7. Fold along line FX and tuck in Z. Repeat on other side. Repeat instructions 1 to 7 for two more sections.

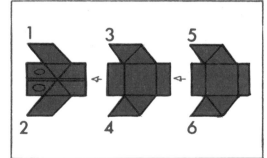

8. Fit the three sections together as shown, and decorate with cotton wool. Bend points 1, 2 up for ears, 3, 4, 5 and 6 down for legs.

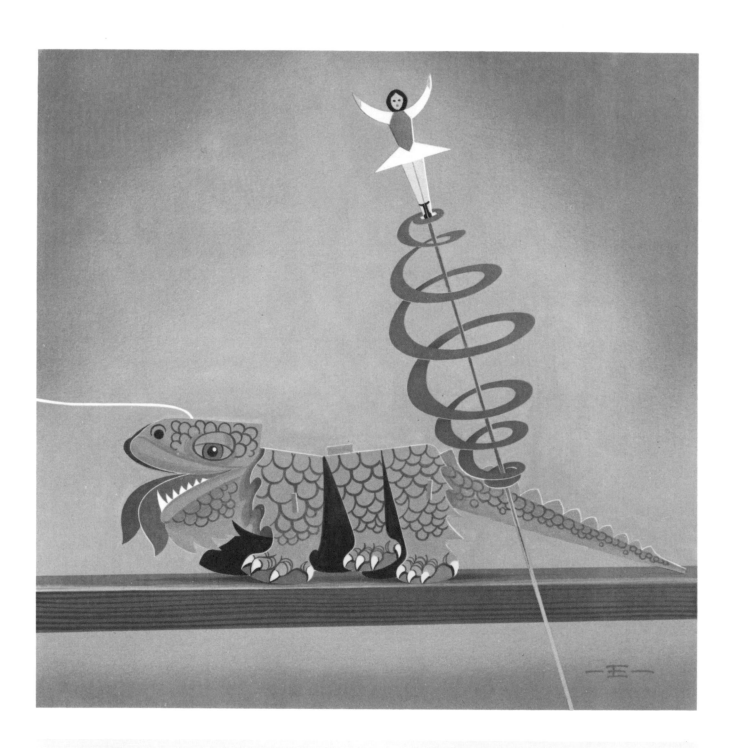

Spinning Spirals

You will need:
Two discs of paper 3" diameter
Cork
Knitting needle
Piece of thin card 2" x 2"
Pencil
Scissors

Walk-Along Dragon

You will need:
Two pieces of thin card
$7\frac{1}{2}$" x 9"
Piece of string
Pencil
Scissors, good penknife
Coloured paints
Glue

Spinning Spirals

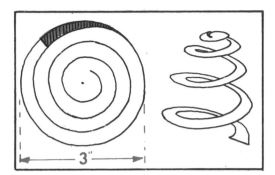

1. Draw two spirals on the paper discs and cut them out.

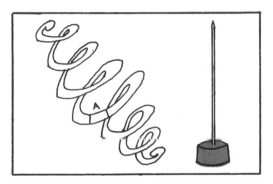

2. Glue the spirals together at A. Stick knitting needle into cork.

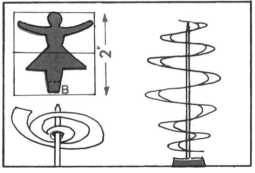

3. Draw and cut out dancer from 2" square of card. Make ¼" hole in centre of one spiral and put needle through.

4. Let needle just prick centre of other spiral. Glue dancer on top and watch her turn!

Walk-Along Dragon

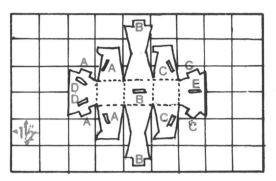

1. Draw pattern on card. Cut it out and make slots where shown.

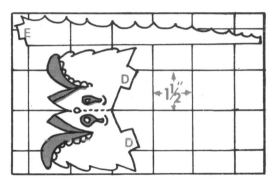

2. Draw and cut patterns on other card for the dragon's head and tail.

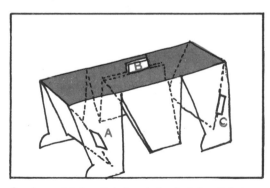

3. Insert tabs A into slots A, tabs B into slots B and tabs C into slots C.

4. Insert and glue tabs D into slots D and tab E into slot E. Attach string to head and pull gently.

Soft Toy

You will need:

Two pieces of coloured felt
9" x 5"
Piece of coloured felt
11½" x 3"
Triangular piece of felt
2½" x 3"

Triangular piece of felt
5" x 3"
Four pieces of coloured felt
3" x 5"
Strip of felt 12" x 1"
Scraps of coloured felt
Cotton wool
Scissors, needle and thread

Soft Toy

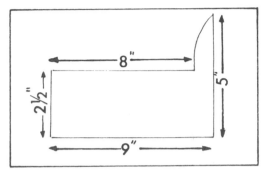

1. Draw and cut the above pattern twice for sides of body.

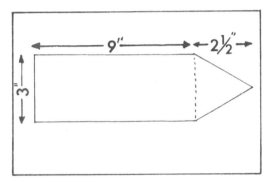

2. Draw and cut pattern for base of soft toy.

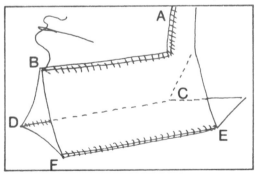

3. Sew two sides together from A to B. Sew sides to base along EF and CD.

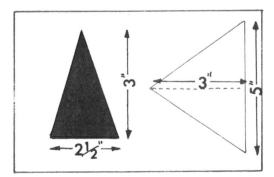

4. Cut two triangular patterns shown above from felt for head.

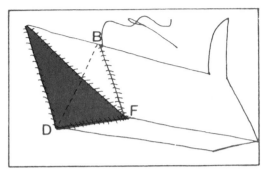

5. Stitch these sections together to form pyramid and sew to body at BFD.

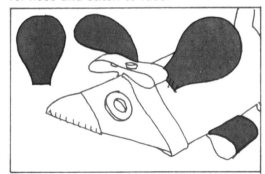

6. Fold over 4 pieces of felt 3″ × 5″, and stitch to body for paws. Cut pattern for nose and stitch to face.

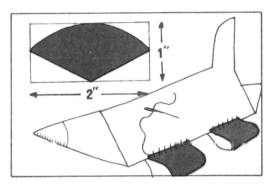

7. Draw and cut patterns for eyes and ears. Sew to body. Take strip 12″ × 1″, stitch around neck and form into bow.

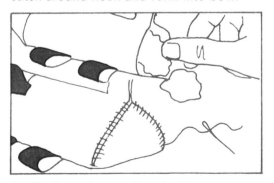

8. Stuff toy from tail end with cotton wool and sew up back flap. Now your soft toy is complete.

Outdoor Noughts & Crosses

You will need:
Four strips of thick card 36" x 1"
Five pieces of card 9" square
Five discs of card 9" diameter
Scissors, good penknife

Whipping Top

You will need:
Cotton reel
3" disc of heavy card
Pencil 3" long
10" piece of dowel
12" of thin string
Glue
Penknife

Outdoor Noughts & Crosses

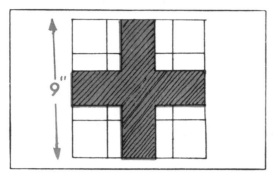

1. Cut out pattern from five pieces of square card to make your crosses.

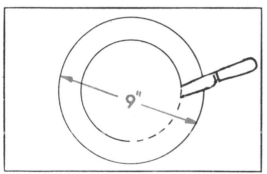

2. Cut centre out of discs as shown to make the noughts for your game.

3. Lay out the strips as shown to make the grid.

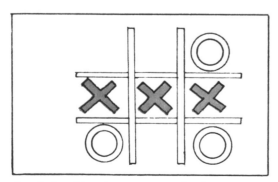

4. Ask a friend to join you. Begin placing the noughts and crosses onto grid. First to get 3 in a row wins.

Whipping Top

1. Make hole in centre of disc and glue reel to it so that holes correspond.

2. Push pencil through reel and disc. Glue it in position with ½" protruding at pointed end.

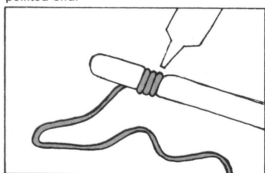

3. Cut a notch in the end of the dowel with a penknife. Tie and glue string to it.

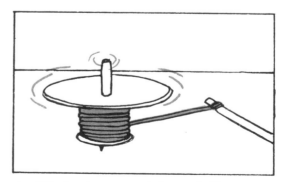

4. Wind string around the reel. Place top on floor. Pull string off with a twist and watch it spin.

Potato Man with Hair that Grows

You will need:
One large potato
Packet of cress seeds
Cotton wool
Good penknife
Coloured paints, water

Rabbit with Ears that Grow

You will need:
Four fresh carrot tops
Empty tin can
Piece white paper to cover
tin can
Enough small stones to almost
fill can
Coloured paints
Glue, water

Potato Man with Hair that Grows

1. Cut off the top and bottom of your potato.

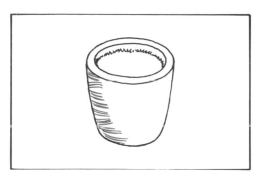

2. Scoop out the top to leave hole about 1" deep. Fill hole with damp cotton wool.

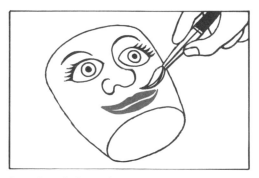

3. Carefully paint a face on the potato.

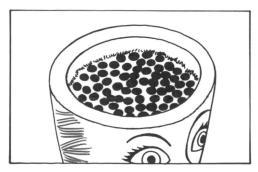

4. Sprinkle the cress seeds on top of the cotton wool and wait for the hair to grow. Remember to keep the cotton wool moist.

Rabbit with Ears that Grow

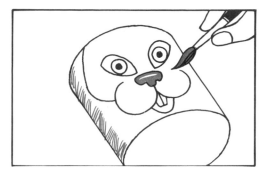

1. Decorate small tin as shown, with rabbit's face.

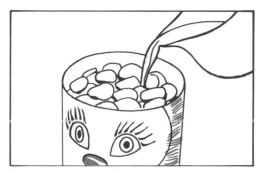

2. Put the small stones in the tin and fill with water.

3. Put two carrot tops on the stones at one side of the tin and two more on the other side.

4. Hold the base of each ear down with stones then watch your rabbit's ears grow. Make sure you keep them well watered.

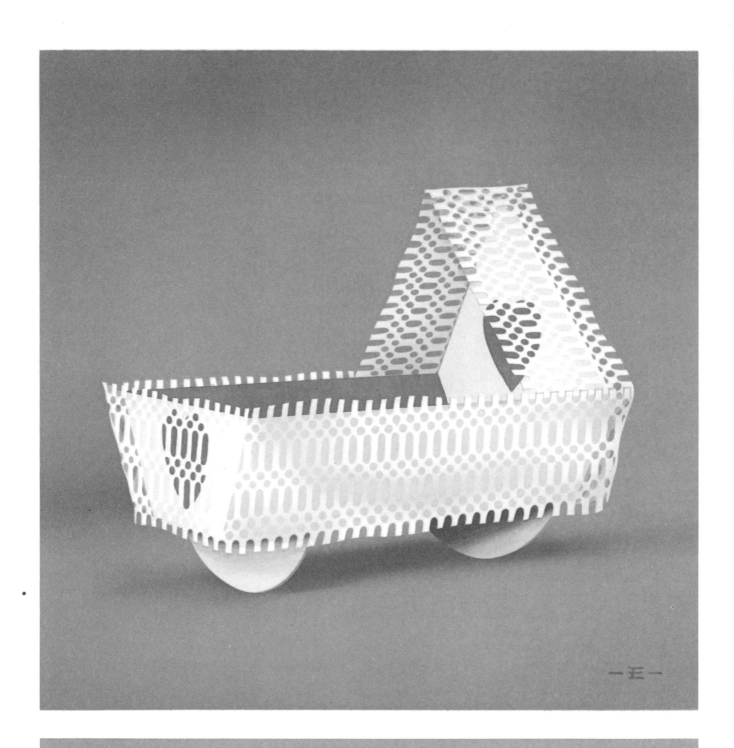

Doll's Cradle

You will need:
Two pieces of cardboard for
rockers 7″ × 2″ (B) and (C)
Piece of cardboard for
headboard 7½″ × 8″ (D)
Piece of cardboard for
footboard 7½″ × 5½″ (E)

Piece of cardboard for base
9½″ × 15″ (A)
Thick wire
Glue and Sellotape
Pencil, scissors
Lace

Doll's Cradle

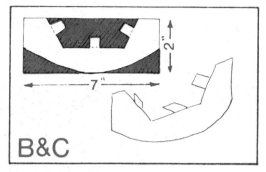

1. Cut two pieces of cardboard as shown to make cradle rockers.

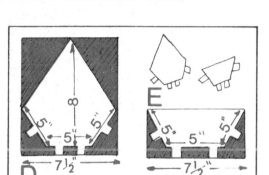

2. Cut the head and foot of the cradle as shown.

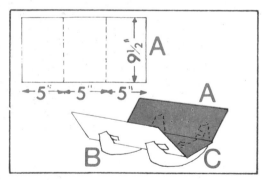

3. Fold piece of cardboard along dotted lines to make base and sides of cradle. Glue on the rockers.

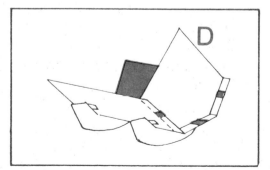

4. Fold tabs down, and glue on the head of the cradle to the base.

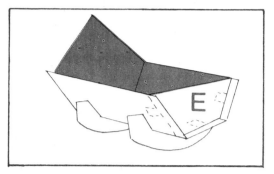

5. Now glue on the foot of the cradle in the same way.

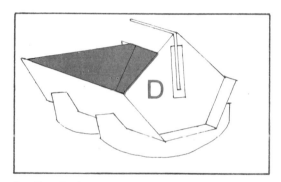

6. Bend wire to shape, and tape it onto headboard of cradle, as shown.

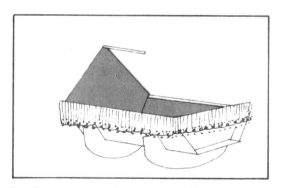

7. Glue strips of lace around the sides and foot of cradle.

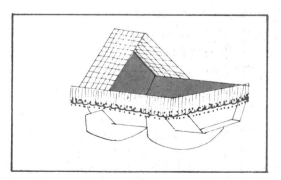

8. Glue on a lace canopy – and your doll's cradle is complete!

Spinner

You will need:

Two cotton reels
2 ft. of thin string
Two cardboard discs 3″ diameter

Pencil
Glue
Good penknife, coloured paints

Spinner

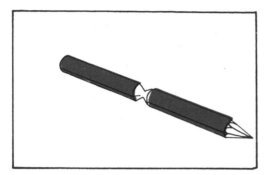

1. Notch the pencil in the middle as shown.

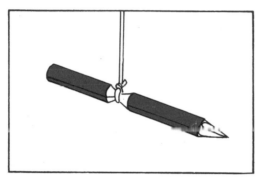

2. Place string in the notch and tie tightly.

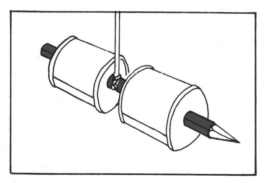

3. Fit two cotton reels tightly on the pencil with a gap of ⅛" left between them at the centre.

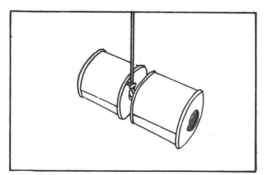

4. Cut off the overlapping pencil ends with a good penknife.

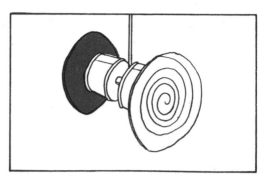

5. Paint designs on cardboard discs and glue them on outside edges of reels.

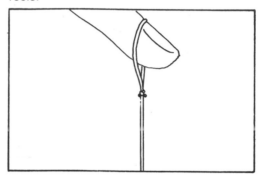

6. Tie a loop in the end of the string to fit your finger through.

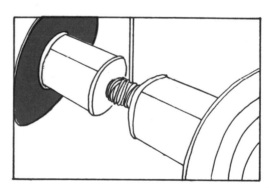

7. Wind string around pencil and allow your spinner to fall.

8. Jerk it upwards when it's at the end of the string to keep it spinning.

Cork Models

You will need:

Six ¼" diameter foil discs
Seven corks
Feathers
Pipe cleaners
Cocktail stick
Drawing pins
Small nail

Penknife
¼" length of coloured drinking straw
Glue, scissors
Paper
Coloured paints

Cork Models

1. Make holes in cork with nail. Push in feathers as shown and two pieces of pipe cleaner to make legs.

2. Push a pipe cleaner into the front of cork for neck. Glue on head feathers and add piece of straw for beak.

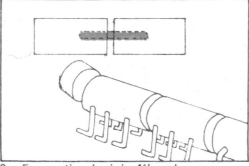

3. For centipede, join 4½ corks together with pipe cleaners. Push six pieces of pipe cleaner into each body cork for legs.

4. Push two pieces of pipe cleaner into head section for horns. Paint and decorate your centipede.

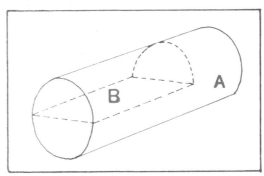

5. To make a galleon cut a cork into two pieces, as shown. Be careful when you are cutting.

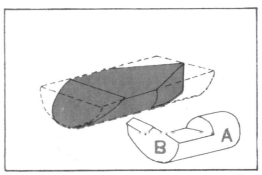

6. Shape piece B with scissors for prow of ship. Glue it to the front of piece A.

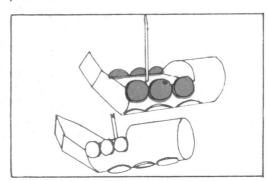

7. Add drawing pins to bottom to weight the keel. Glue foil discs to sides for shields.

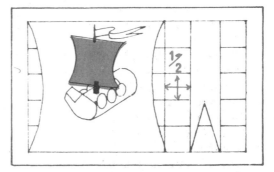

8. Cut patterns from paper for sail and flag. Push cocktail stick into hull then fix them into position. Watch it float.

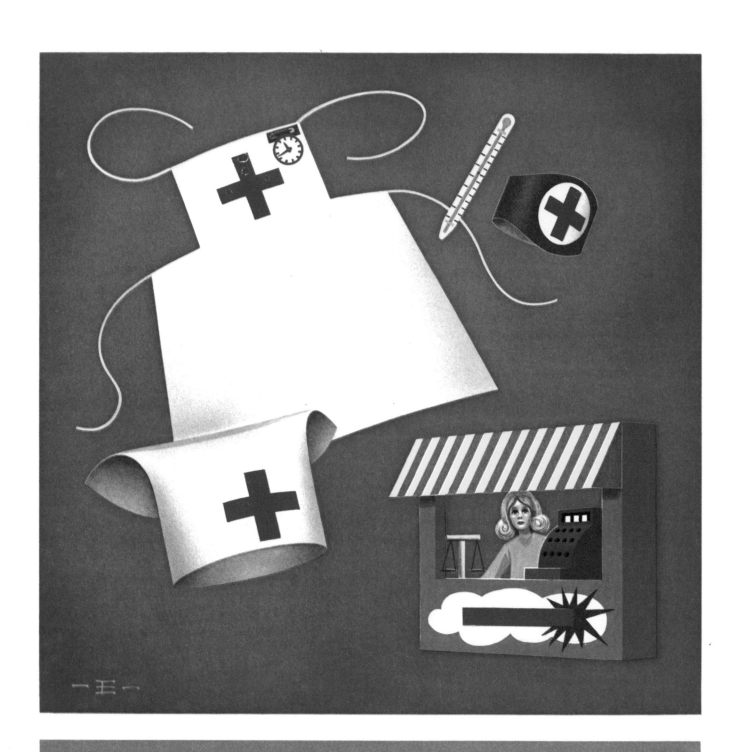

Doll's Shop

You will need:
Sheet of thin card 12″ x 15″
(A)
Strip of thin card 13″ x 2″
Piece of thin card 4½″ x 3″
Dowel 1½″ long x 1/8″ dia.
Drinking straw
One pin
Two discs of paper ½″
diameter
Disc of paper 1″ diameter
Glue
Pencil, scissors, needle and
thread, coloured paints

Nurse's Outfit

You will need:
Piece of thin card 13″ x 25″
Piece of thin white card, or
white material 18″ x 24″
Four cloth tapes 36″ long
x ½″ wide
Piece of card for watch,
armband and thermometer
Glue
Pencil, scissors, coloured
paints

Doll's Shop

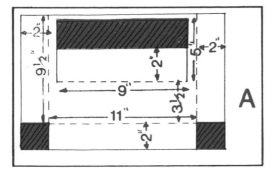

1. Draw and cut out pattern for shop front from card 12″ × 15″. Fold on dotted lines.

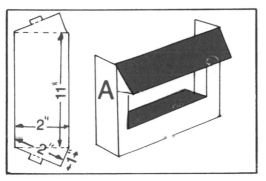

2. Cut out the roof from card 13″ × 2″. Fold and glue it onto shop front. Paint with bright colours.

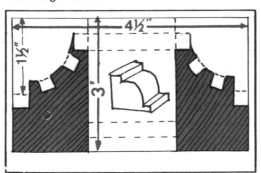

3. Cut pattern from piece of card 4½″ × 3″ to make cash register. Fold and glue tabs inside.

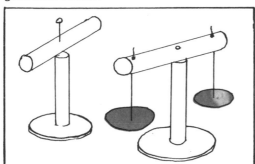

4. Pin straw to dowel. Thread ½″ discs and glue dowel to 1″ base disc to make shop scales.

Nurse's Outfit

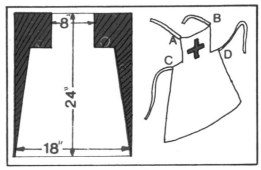

1. Draw and cut out pattern for apron. Glue on tapes as shown, at A, B, C and D.

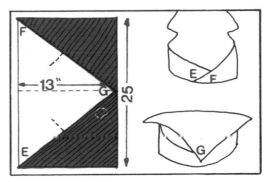

2. Cut pattern for cap. Cut along dotted lines, then glue E and F together. Bring G down to join them.

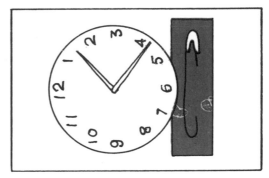

3. Draw and cut pattern for watch. Pin onto top of apron.

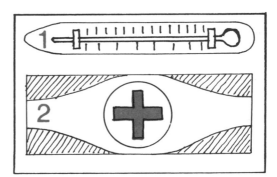

4. Draw and cut patterns for thermometer and armband. Then decorate as shown.

Colour Spin

You will need:
Disc of stiff card 3" diameter
2 ft. of thin string
Scissors, coloured paints

Carousel

You will need:
Disc of stiff paper 16" diameter
Two discs of stiff card 6" diameter
Pencil, sharpened at both ends
Cork
Strip of stiff paper
Sheets of coloured paper
Glue and Sellotape
Scissors, coloured paints

Colour Spin

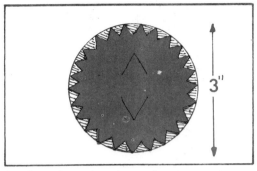

1. Cut triangular pieces from the outside of the disc, as shown.

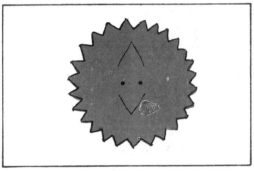

2. Make 2 small holes, ⅛″ on each side of the centre of the disc. Cut V shaped notches where indicated.

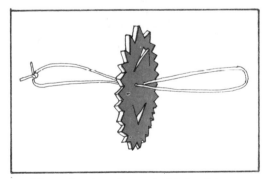

3. Thread string through. Make 2 loops as shown, and tie ends together.

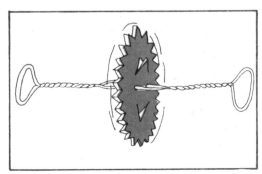

4. Hold a loop in each hand. Twist the disc to wind the string. Then pull the string and make it spin.

Carousel

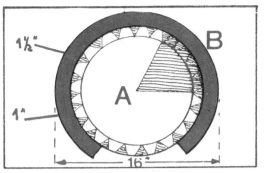

1. Cut out the red and shaded areas shown on the 16″ disc of paper. Save outer piece (B) for later.

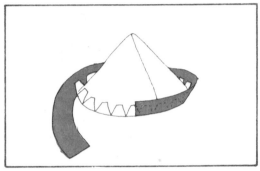

2. Fold and glue (A) into a cone. Fold tabs upwards, and glue strip of paper (B) around outside.

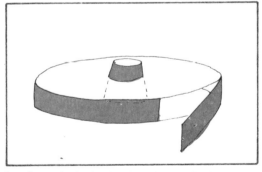

3. Cut a hole in the 6″ disc to fit the cork. Glue other disc to base. Glue paper strip around base.

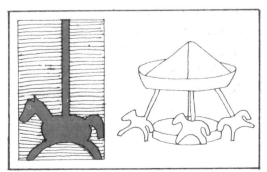

4. Cut paper horses and stick on as shown. Push one end of pencil in cork, balance roundabout on other.

Magic Tree

You will need:
Large piece of green paper
(newspaper will do)
Sellotape
Scissors

Elephant Wall Frieze

You will need:
Three strips of coloured
paper 12″ × 3″
Drawing pins
Ruler
Pencil
Scissors, coloured paints

Magic Tree

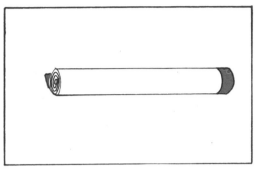

1. Roll paper into a tight tube and tape end as shown.

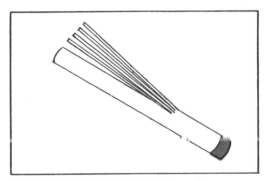

2. Cut down the tube to make strips, to within about 4″ from the taped end.

3. Keep doing this until you have cut strips all around the tube.

4. Bend strips down and pull upwards from centre. Watch your tree grow.

Elephant Wall Frieze

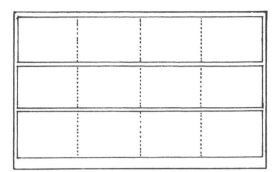

1. Mark the pattern above on your 12″ × 3″ paper strip and fold along the dotted lines.

2. Fold each piece of paper into 4 as shown, and draw elephants on the top of each folded piece.

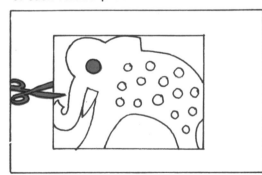

3. Cut out the patterns. Make sure that there is an uncut piece at each side.

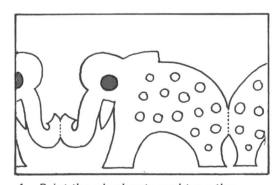

4. Paint the elephants and tape the three strips together. Pin the coloured friezes along the top of your wall.

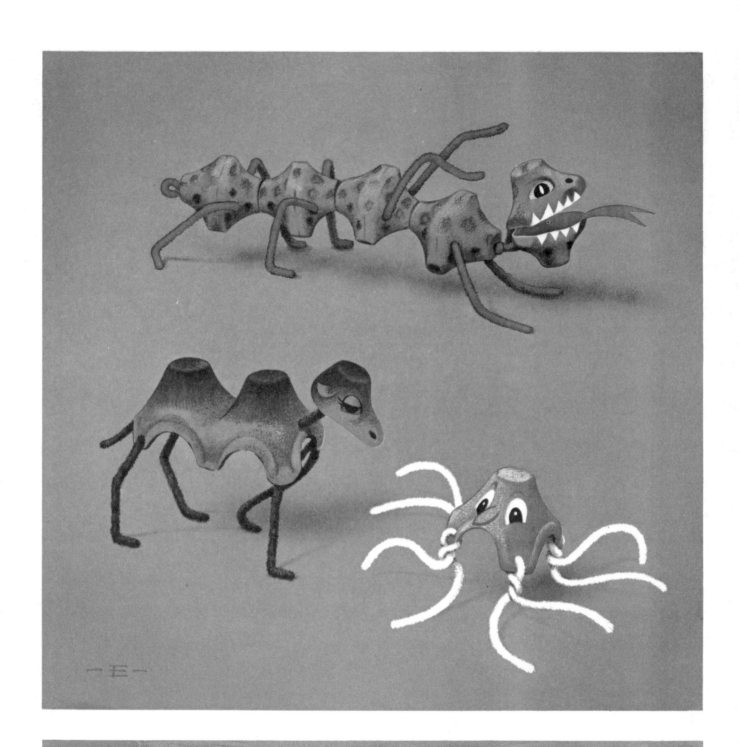

Egg Box Models

You will need:
Egg boxes
Pipe cleaners
Glue or Sellotape

Good penknife, scissors
coloured paints

Egg Box Models

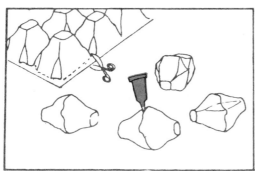

1. Cut eight segments from egg boxes and glue them together in pairs.

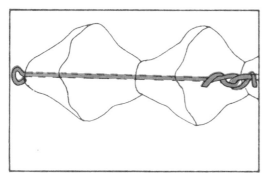

2. Pierce holes in ends and thread four sections together with pipe cleaners.

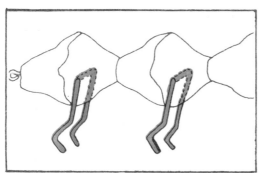

3. Pierce holes in sides of each section. Insert pipe cleaners and bend to make legs.

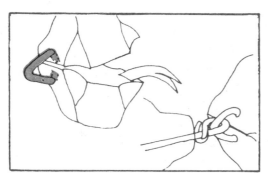

4. Cut 2 more segments and hinge together with pipe cleaner for head. Join to body as shown.

5. Cut pattern for tongue from box and glue to mouth. Paint and decorate your egg box dragon.

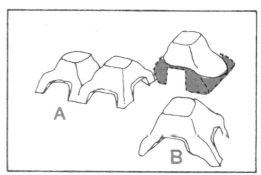

6. To make a camel (A) and an octopus (B), cut your egg box as shown.

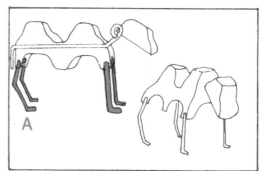

7. Join head to body of camel with a pipe cleaner. Make holes at sides and insert pipe cleaners for legs.

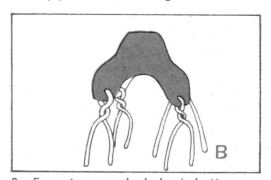

8. For octopus make holes in bottom corners. Insert cleaners and twist to make tentacles. Decorate camel and octopus with paints.

Kaleidoscope

You will need:
Stiff card 12″ long × 6½″ wide
Tin foil 12″ long × 6″ wide
Piece of card 3½″ square
Piece of card 3″ square
Two pieces of "Cellophane" 3″
square

Glue and Sellotape
White paint
Transparent coloured beads
Pencil scissors, good
penknife

Kaleidoscope

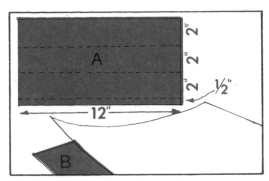

1. Draw dotted lines on one side of 12″ × 6½″ card in positions shown, and glue tin foil on other side.

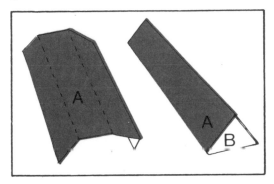

2. Bend along lines so that foil is inside. Glue flap outside.

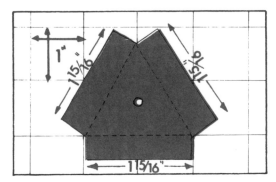

3. Draw and cut out pattern from 3″ square of card. Make small peephole in centre.

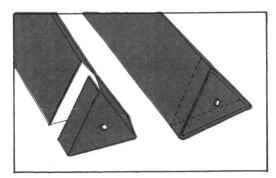

4. Glue tabs inside one end of triangular tube.

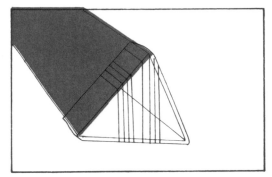

5. Carefully glue a piece of clear "Cellophane" over the other end of the tube.

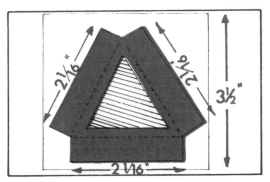

6. Draw and cut pattern from 3½″ square of card. Cut triangular 'window' with good penknife.

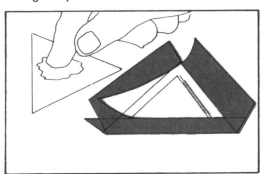

7. Carefully glue a triangle of "Cellophane" over window. Rub a dab of white paint on outside when glue is dry.

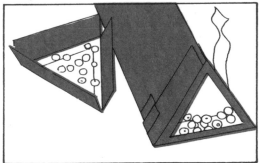

8. Put coloured beads in this cup and tape it to end of tube. Shake gently. Look through peephole.

Jacob's Ladder

You will need:
Twelve pieces of very thick
card 3″ × 2″
Five yards of ½″ wide cloth
tape

Glue
Scissors
Coloured paints

Jacob's Ladder

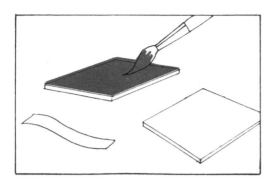

1. Paint one side of each card blue and the other red. Cut tape into 40 pieces 4½" long.

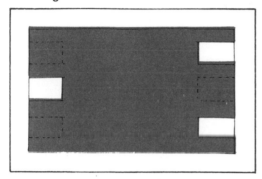

2. Mark cards on red sides as shown. Mark on blue sides at opposite edges. (See dotted lines.)

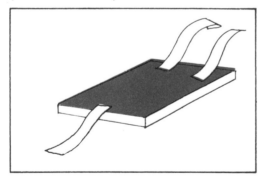

3. Glue three strips of tape onto every red side but one.

4. Take tapes under each card and glue to the marks on blue side of the next card.

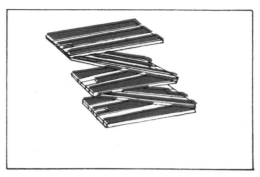

5. Join all the cards in this way, leaving the card with no tapes until last. Leave glue to set.

6. Fold the ladder. Then take the two top steps and open the ladder.

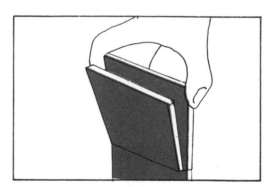

7. Open two top steps and hold with finger and thumb as shown.

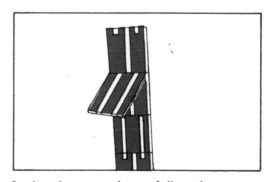

8. Let the second step fall, and see what happens!

GIFTS AND DECORATIONS

Clothes Peg-Bag

You will need:
Wire coat hanger
Piece of strong cloth
32″ x 16″

Two pieces of coloured
ribbon 9″ long
Scissors, needle and thread

Clothes Peg-Bag

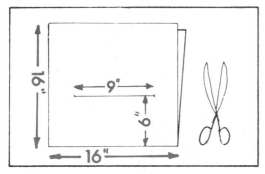

1. Fold the cloth in half. Cut a 9″ slit as shown in one of the 16″ squares.

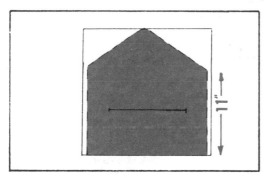

2. Sew both squares together, along dotted lines, with the best side inwards.

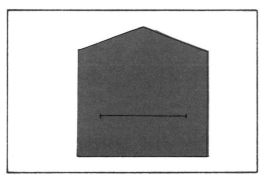

3. Cut off excess cloth, and turn bag inside out.

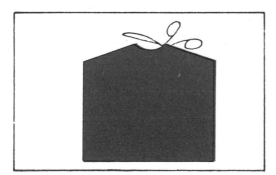

4. Make a small hole in the top for the hook of the coat hanger.

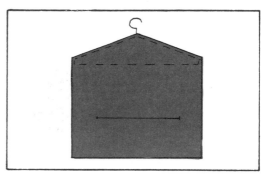

5. Put hanger inside bag through slit, and push hook through hole at top of bag.

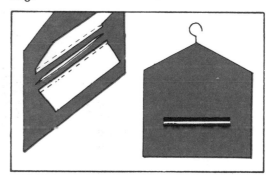

6. Sew the edges of the ribbons to the edges of the slits. Sew inside and outside.

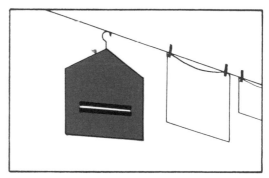

7. Your bag is now ready to fill with pegs and hang on the line.

8. You can also use your bag to keep your toys or shoes in.

Bookmark

You will need:
Piece of coloured ribbon 8''
long x 1½'' wide or thin
card
Pieces of coloured paper or
cloth
Glue
Pencil, scissors

Felt Oven Gloves

You will need:
Six pieces of thick felt,
9'' long x 7½'' wide
Scraps of coloured cloth
Cotton wool for stuffing
Cloth tape 18'' long x ½''
wide
Scissors, needle and thread

Bookmark

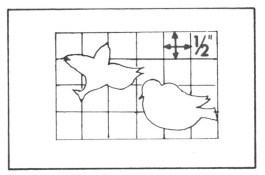

1. Cut designs from coloured paper or cloth in the above shapes.

2. Begin glueing them onto the ribbon or thin card.

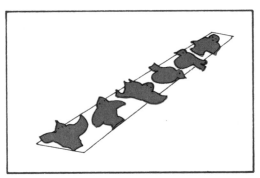

3. When you have covered the ribbon or card your bookmark is complete.

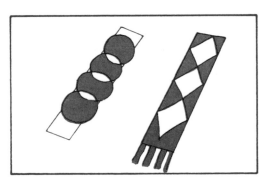

4. You can make more bookmarks using different shapes. Allow glue to dry before you put it in a book!

Felt Oven Gloves

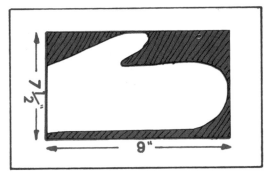

1. Cut six felt patterns as shown. Stitch two pairs along the edges. Add one more to palm of each glove.

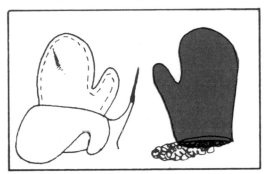

2. Turn gloves inside out. Then stuff palms of gloves with cotton wool and sew together.

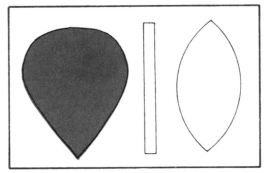

3. Cut petals and leaf shapes from scraps of coloured cloth. Sew them onto top of each glove.

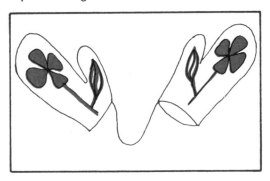

4. Sew ends of 18″ cloth tape to each glove, just below the thumb.

'Snakey' the Draft Excluder

You will need:
Piece of cloth 36" long
x 12" wide
Four pieces of cloth 9"
long x 6" wide
(different colours)
Rags for stuffing
Two buttons
Scraps of coloured cloth
Scissors, needle and thread

Desk Tidy

You will need:
Plastic detergent bottle
Three pieces of thick card
3½" square
Piece of thick card 5½"
square for head
Glue
Pencil, scissors, good
penknife, coloured paints

42

'Snakey' the Draft Excluder

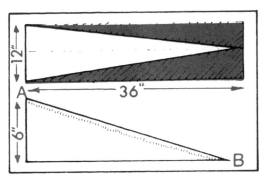

1. Cut out pattern for body, as shown. Fold and sew from A to B. Then turn inside out.

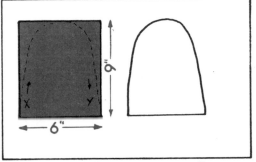

2. Cut 9" × 6" pieces to pattern. Sew two pieces together. Repeat, and turn both inside out. These are the head pieces.

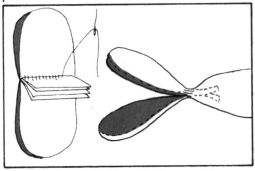

3. Stuff body and head pieces with rags. Then sew head pieces together, insert head flaps into body and stitch across neck.

4. Sew on buttons for eyes, and other scraps of coloured cloth for decoration.

Desk Tidy

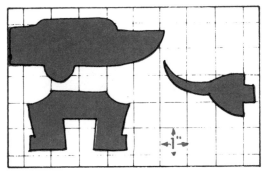

1. Draw and cut patterns on cards for legs, head and tail. Cut section from one side of bottle as shown below.

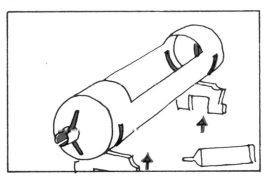

2. Cut slots in sides of bottle for legs and in top and bottom for head and tail. Glue on legs as shown.

3. Push head into top and secure with glue.

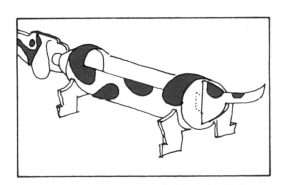

4. Push tail into bottom of bottle. Paint your holder and fill it with pencils.

Table Decoration

You will need:

Plastic detergent bottle
Piece of thick card 12" x 10"
Three discs of white paper
10" diameter
Glass tumbler

Candle
Tin foil
Glue and Sellotape
Scissors, good penknife
Green paint

44

Table Decoration

1. Draw and cut pattern for leaf base from thick card 12″ × 10″.

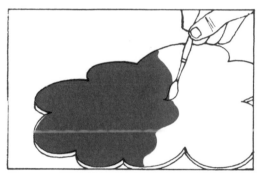

2. Paint the leaf base green and leave to dry.

3. Draw and cut pattern above from three 10″ diameter discs of white paper. Curl up ends of petals, as shown.

4. Arrange and glue the 3 petal shapes together to make the finished flower. Glue them to centre of leaf base.

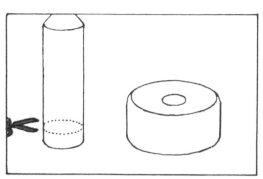

5. Cut the base from a plastic bottle 1″ from the bottom for holder. Make hole in it to fit candle.

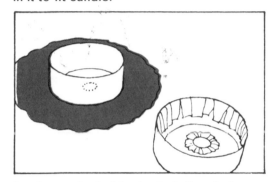

6. Cover the holder in tin foil and glue overlap inside.

7. Glue holder inside glass tumbler. Stand tumbler in centre of flower, as shown.

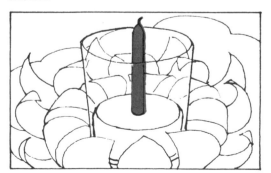

8. Push a candle into the holder and place your decoration in the centre of the table.

Montage Picture Calendar

You will need:
Piece of coloured cardboard
18" x 15"
Piece of paper 14" x 10"
Scraps of coloured paper
Calendar
Glue
Scissors, pencil

Pop-Up Card

You will need:
Piece of card 16" x 10"
Pencil, good penknife,
coloured paints

Montage Picture Calendar

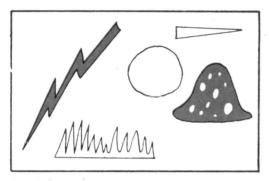

1. Draw and cut out shapes from coloured paper as shown.

2. Cut out some more shapes, in different colours.

3. Arrange them in groups, and glue then onto the paper.

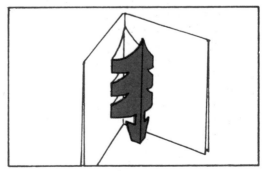

4. When your picture is finished, glue paper onto card and glue calendar underneath. Attach string to hang it up.

Pop-Up Card

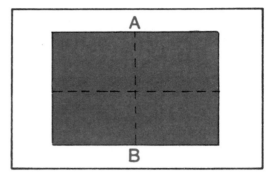

1. Fold card in half, along line A to B.

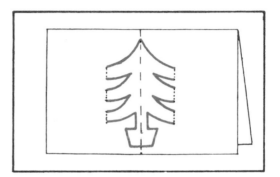

2. Draw tree in centre of card. Cut along red lines – but leave the ends of branches uncut.

3. Push Christmas tree towards you, and fold the centre crease the other way. Now close the card.

4. Paint and decorate the tree. Write on the words 'Merry Christmas' and a Christmas message.

Paper Mats

You will need:
Two different coloured
pieces of paper, one
14″ x 10″, the other
12″ x 10″
Glue
Ruler
Pencil
Scissors

Windmill

You will need:
Coloured paper disc 8″
diameter
Twelve long strips for
streamers ¼″ wide
¼″ dowel about 2 ft. long
Wire about 6″ long
Disc of paper ¾″ diameter
Drinking straw
Sellotape
Pencil, scissors, pliers

Paper Mats

Windmill

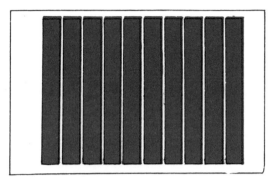

1. Draw and cut 10 pieces of coloured paper 1″ wide by 14″ long and 12 pieces 1″ wide by 12″ long.

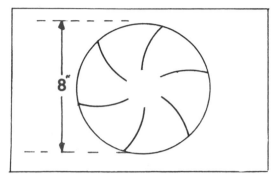

1. Draw and cut pattern as shown. Leave space in the centre.

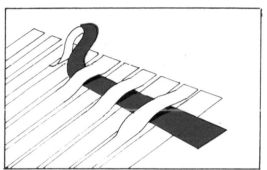

2. Weave the 14″ strips between the 12″ strips as shown.

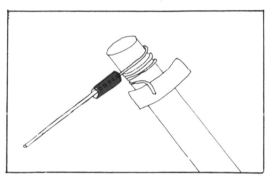

2. Bend wire as shown. Tape it to the stick. Cut ½″ of drinking straw and fit over wire.

3. Carry on weaving until you have used all the strips.

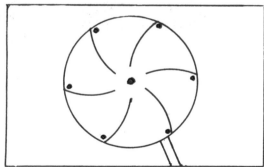

3. Make holes in the windmill as shown. Push end of wire through centre hole.

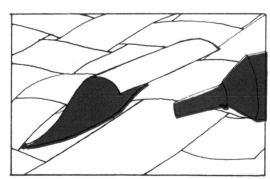

4. Then put a little glue where the strips meet at the end.

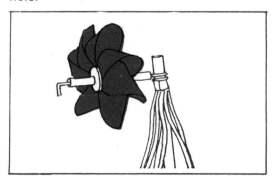

4. Bend fins to centre and fit outside holes on wire. Add ¾″ disc, then ½″ straw and bend wire over. Tape streamers to stick.

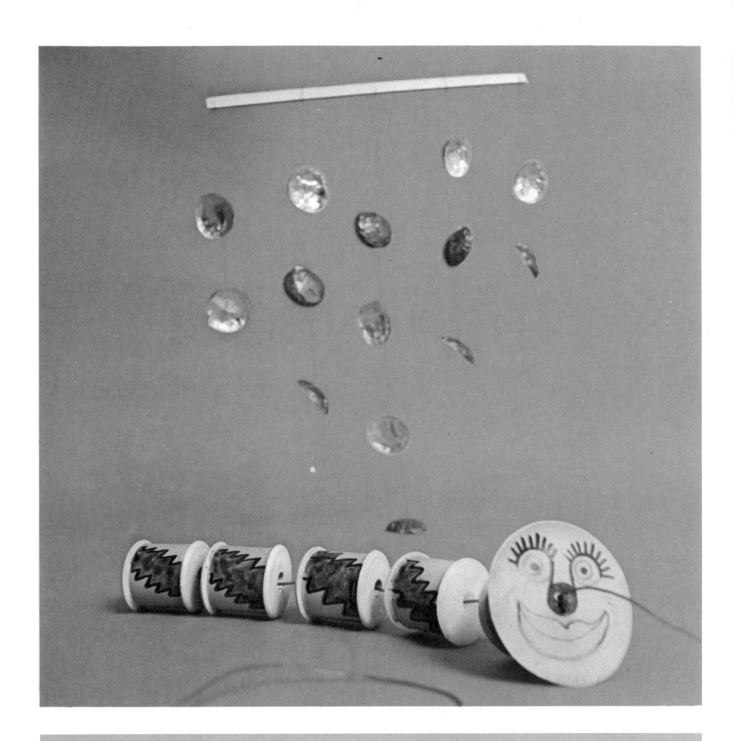

Cotton Reel Caterpillar

You will need:
Five cotton reels
Thick card disc 2½″
diameter
Thick card disc 1″
diameter
Piece white paper 5″ square
to cover reels
9″ length of elastic
Two small buttons
Thin string (approx 1 yard)
Glue, pencil, good penknife
Coloured paints

Bottle Top Mobile

You will need:
Fourteen metal foil
bottle tops
Piece thick card ½″ x 12″
5′ length black cotton
2′ length black cotton

50

Cotton Reel Caterpillar

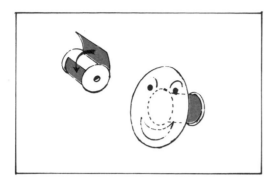

1. Cover reels with white paper. Paint face on large card disc and glue one reel to centre of other side.

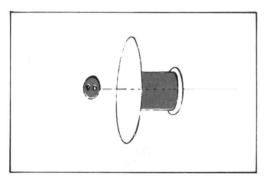

2. Pierce hole in centre of face. Tie elastic to one button and thread other end through hole.

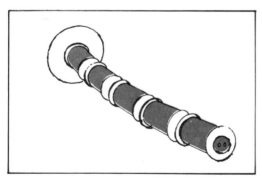

3. Thread on remaining reels. Tie end to other button. Decorate body reels.

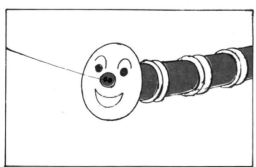

4. Tie end of string to button on face. Pull your caterpillar along and watch him wriggle.

Bottle Top Mobile

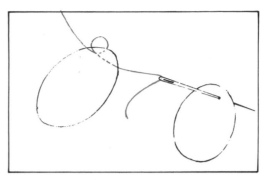

1. Smooth out creases in the bottle tops and using needle, thread each one with your needle onto 5 ft of cotton.

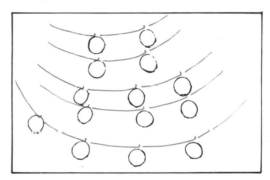

2. Space tops evenly along the cotton and cut two lengths 8", two lengths 10½" and one length 17".

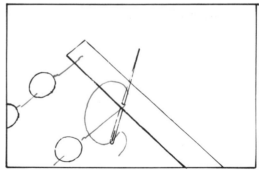

3. Sew one end of each strand onto the card.

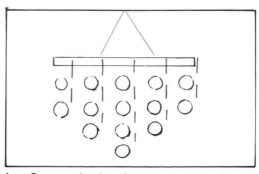

4. Secure the bottle tops by knotting the free ends. Then trim off any excess. Sew a 2 ft length of cotton to the middle of the card and hang your mobile up.

Party Place Names

You will need:
Piece of thick paper 5″ x 7″
for each guest
Ruler, coloured paints
Scissors, pencil

Party Sweet Tree

You will need:
One paper or plastic cup full
of earth
Small branch
Cotton
Wrapped sweets
Coloured paints or silver foil

Party Place Names

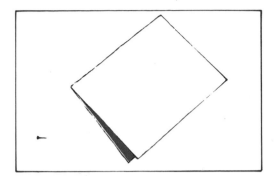

1. Fold paper in half.

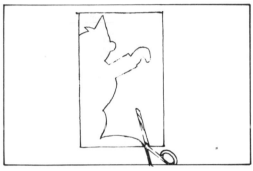

2. Draw the outline of your clown with his back to the fold. Cut round the shape but do not cut along the fold.

3. Paint both sides of your clown and write the name of one of your guests on his shirt.

4. Make a different coloured clowns for each guest. Hang the clowns onto the sides of your guests' glasses.

Party Sweet Tree

1. Decorate cup with paints or cover with silver foil. Fill with earth.

2. Push the small branch firmly into the earth.

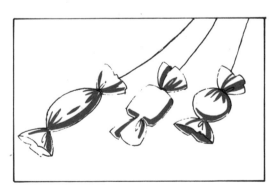

3. Tie short length of cotton to the end of each sweet.

4. Hang the sweets on the "tree". Make sure there are enough sweets for all your friends.

Rose

You will need:

Green and red crepe paper

Glue

Sellotape

Thin wire

Thin card

Scissors

Sturdy wire (flexible)

Rose

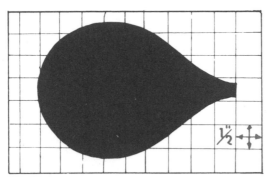

1. Draw and cut pattern above from card for petal shape.

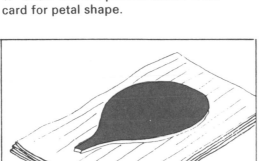

2. Fold crepe paper to eight thicknesses. Cut 16 petal shapes using card outline. Make sure grain of paper is vertical.

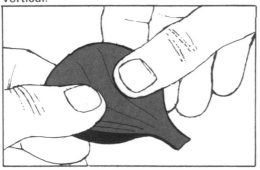

3. Stretch 4 of the crepe petals in the centre to form a hollow.

4. Stretch another 4 petals to make a slightly smaller hollow.

5. Take 4 more petals and make a very small hollow in these.

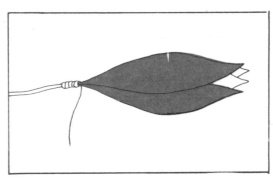

6. Take your last 4 petals and wrap at the top of your wire stem as shown. Attach at base with thin wire.

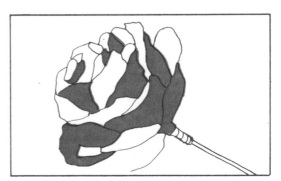

7. Add other petals, flattest first, until rose is complete. Secure with thin wire.

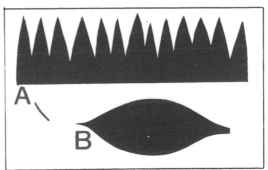

8. Draw and cut patterns shown from green crepe. Wrap A around bottom of rose and tape B onto stem for leaves. Paint stem green.

Sunflower

You will need:
Cardboard disc 6″ diameter
Three 14″ squares of yellow
paper
2 ft. of ¼″ dowel - or tree
twig
Ball of dark brown wool
Glue
Sellotape
Scissors

Dahlia

You will need:
Three discs of coloured
paper 5″ diameter
9″ piece of wire
Green paper for leaves
Glue
Pencil, scissors, Sellotape

Sunflower

Dahlia

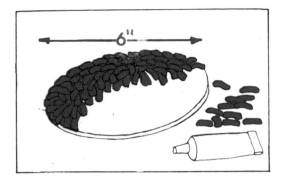

1. Cut wool into short lengths, approx. ½". Glue pieces to one side of 6" disc.

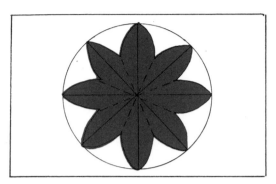

1. Draw and cut pattern for flower. Fold along solid lines.

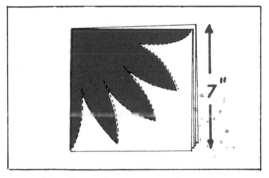

2. Fold yellow tissue paper into 7" squares. Cut pattern from open sides for petals and open out.

2. Open out, turn over and fold along dotted lines as shown.

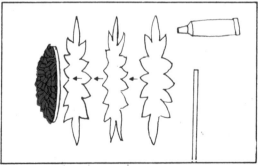

3. Glue the three pieces of yellow tissue paper to back of disc and arrange as shown.

3. Make 2 more. Thread wire through centres and bend down to secure. Arrange petals to make completed flower.

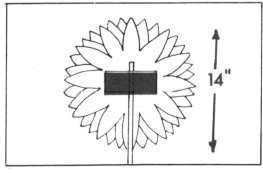

4. Tape stick or branch to back of flower.

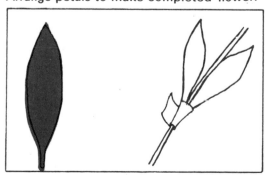

4. Draw and cut pattern for leaves and tape to stem.

Lantern

You will need:
Coloured paper 18″ × 8″
Disc of coloured paper 12″
diameter
Wool
Glue
Pencil, ruler, scissors

Paper Necklace

You will need:
An old coloured magazine
Glue
Thread
Scissors or good penknife
Knitting needle

Lantern

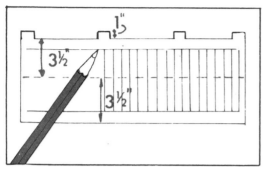

1. Draw pattern above on paper. Draw vertical lines ½" apart, as shown.

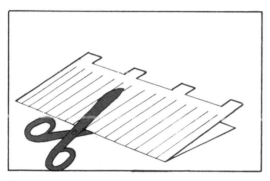

2. Fold along the dotted line and cut as shown.

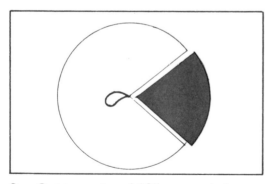

3. Cut to centre of 12" paper circle. Cut out segment, add knotted loop of wool, then glue to make cone.

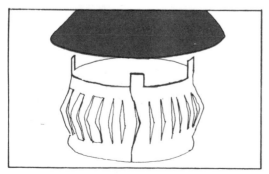

4. Open the paper strip and glue ends together. Then tape tabs inside top. Hang lantern up.

Paper Necklace

1. Mark and cut 18 triangular shapes from a coloured magazine picture 1" at the base and 10" long.

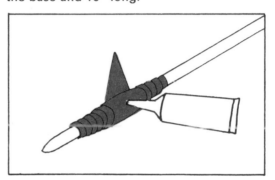

2. Put the large end of the triangle around a knitting needle. Roll it up and glue the point.

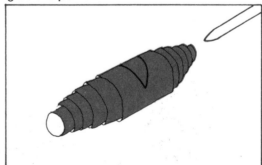

3. Hold until glue sets then pull needle out. This is one bead. Now make another 17 beads.

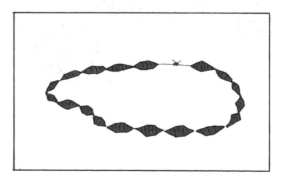

4. When all your beads are made, push the thread through them and tie the ends together.

ARTS AND CRAFTS

Potato Prints

You will need:
Potatoes – medium or large ones
Paper
Coloured paints
Penknife

Leaf Prints

You will need:
Various shaped leaves
Large sheet of white paper
Smaller piece of cardboard
Coloured paints

Potato Prints

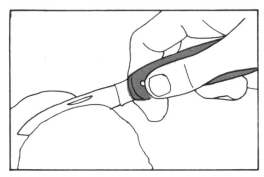

1. Cut a potato in half. Try to make sure that the cut is straight.

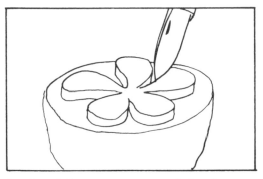

2. Carefully cut away part of the flat surface to leave a pattern or a letter.

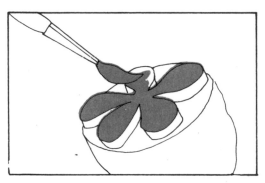

3. Brush paint onto the raised pattern or letter. Use whatever colour you like, but not too much.

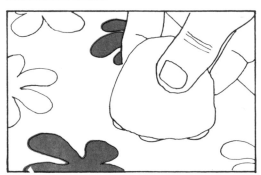

4. Press the potato on the paper. Use other designs and colours until your pattern is finished.

Leaf Prints

1. Collect as many different leaves as you can. If they are crinkly, flatten them in a book.

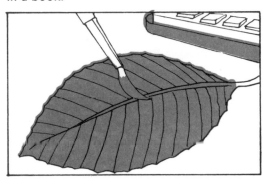

2. Take one leaf and paint it one colour. Don't put too much paint on!

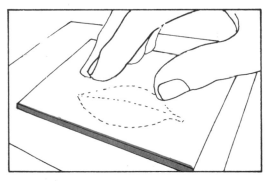

3. Let the paint get fairly dry. Use card to press the leaf, painted side down, on paper.

4. Paint more leaves in different colours. Press them on the paper until your picture is complete.

Silver Bird

You will need:
Thin card 8" x 5"
Newspapers
Roll of tin foil
Thick cardboard 17" x 6" for base

Two pieces of thin card 5" x 2"
Two large paper clips
Sellotape
Scissors
Paint, glue

Silver Bird

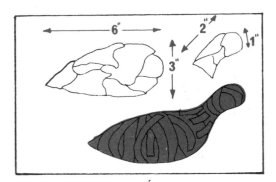

1. Crumble sheets of newspaper and bind them with tape to form the body and head of the bird.

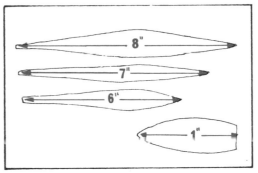

2. Cut patterns from card 8″×5″ for tail and body feather guides. Use these guides to cut the feathers from foil.

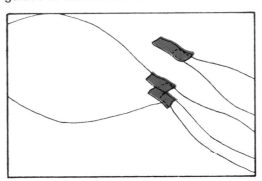

3. Tape two of each size tail feather to the end of the body, beginning with the longest.

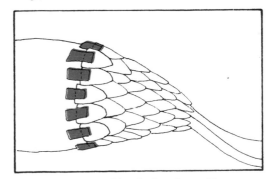

4. Cut dozens of body feathers. Tape them on as shown, beginning at the tail.

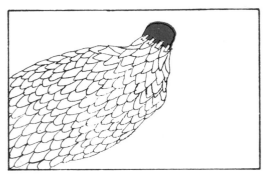

5. Continue until the whole body is covered. Leave area uncovered at top of neck.

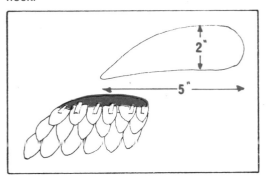

6. Draw and cut two patterns for wings from cards 5″×2″. Tape feathers to wings as shown, then tape wings to body.

7. Draw and cut pattern from foil for head. Fold along dotted line. Tape to neck. Glue on foil discs for eyes.

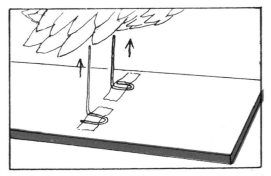

8. Straighten clips to make legs. Tape to baseboard in position. Push bird onto the two upright wires. Paint base.

Three Dimensional Picture

You will need:
Piece of thick cardboard
20" x 14"
Old boxes, tins, pieces of
wood, etc.
Strong glue
Coloured paint

Mosaic Pictures

You will need:
Coloured magazines
Piece of thin card 10" x 8"
Scissors
Eraser
Pencil
Glue

Three Dimensional Picture

1. Put the board on a flat surface. Put the scraps of wood, boxes and tins on the board.

2. Move them around until they form an interesting pattern.

3. Now glue each piece in position.

4. Choose a bright colour and paint the base and the pieces. Paint the tops of some shapes a different colour.

Mosaic Pictures

1. Lightly draw the outline for your picture in pencil on a piece of thin card 10″ × 8″.

2. Remove coloured pictures from magazines and cut them into ¼″ squares.

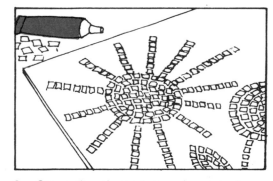

3. Group the pieces into colours and begin sticking them onto your picture until each shape is filled in.

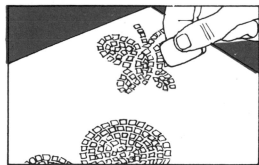

4. Erase the pencil outline to complete your mosaic picture.

'Lace' Picture Frame

You will need:
A picture or photograph
A much larger piece of
coloured paper
Paper doilies
Paste
Scissors

Felt Pictures

You will need:
A piece of white cardboard
Scraps of coloured felt or
cloth
Glue
Pencil
Scissors

'Lace' Picture Frame

1. Take your favourite picture or photograph from a magazine and cut it out.

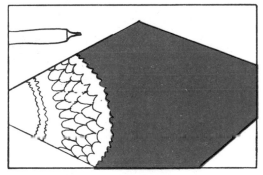

2. Fold and cut a paper doily into four equal parts. Paste these in corners of coloured paper.

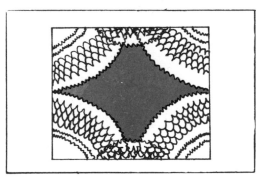

3. Cut pieces from other doilies to complete edge of frame.

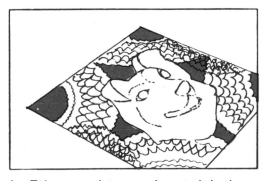

4. Take your picture and paste it in the middle of your 'lace' frame.

Felt Pictures

1. Your first felt picture could be an owl. Draw him on the cardboard like this.

2. Cut the coloured felt into shapes to match the different parts of your drawing.

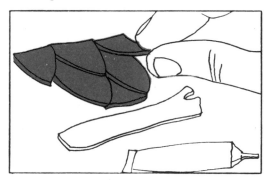

3. Stick on the feathers, beginning at the bottom, until you reach the head.

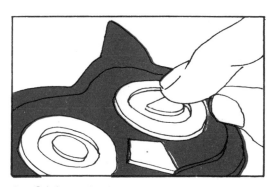

4. Stick on the head. Use circles for eyes. Try making more felt pictures of different animals.

Collage Pictures

You will need:

Sheet of paper or card
Wool
Cloth
Cotton wool
Coloured paper
Pipe cleaners

Straw
Small flowers or petals
Grass
Small leaves
Glue
Pencil, scissors

Collage Pictures

1. Draw a picture on the paper as a pattern.

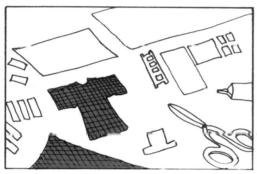

2. Cut cloth to make clothes, coloured paper for house, ladder, cart etc.

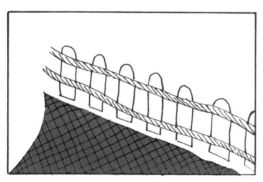

3. Make fence with paper and wool, and stick onto your drawing. Stick on green cloth for field.

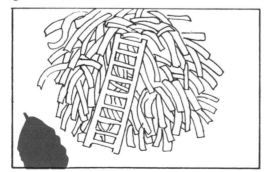

4. Use straw for the haystacks and glue on the ladder.

5. Make sheep by gluing cotton wool onto pipe cleaner shape, as shown.

6. Make the scarecrow as shown, and glue him in the field.

7. Glue on large pieces of paper for house. Use smaller pieces for windows, doors and chimney.

8. Stick on the flowers, leaves, cotton wool clouds and grass until your collage picture is complete.

Pom Pom Cat

You will need:
Ball of wool
Two cardboard discs 3″
diameter
Scraps of coloured paper
Glue
Thin string or thread
Scissors, darning needle

French Knitting

You will need:
Ball of wool
Cotton reel
Four nails ½″ long with
small heads
Hammer, knitting needle

Pom Pom Cat

French Knitting

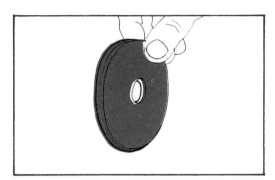

1. Cut ½″ diameter holes in the centres of the cardboard discs.

1. Hammer 4 nails into one end of cotton reel, as shown.

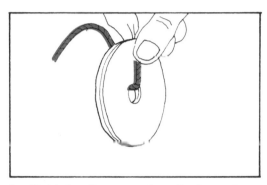

2. Hold the discs together. Push wool through centre holes, holding the ends together, as shown.

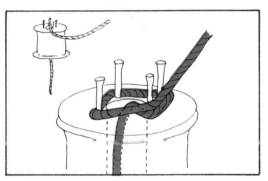

2. Push wool through hole in reel, then wind it around nails until you are back at first nail.

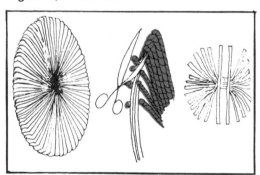

3. Wrap wool around the discs until full. Cut as shown, and tie tightly in centre before removing cards.

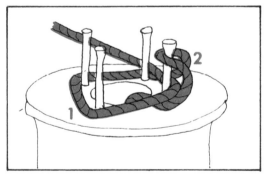

3. Lift bottom strand 2 over top of strand 1. Loop it over nail with knitting needle.

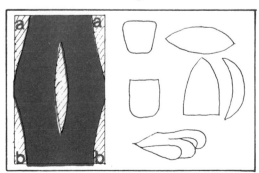

4. Cut above pattern and fold for paw. Add other shapes for eyes, nose, mouth, tongue and ears. Glue onto cat.

4. Continue doing this round the nails and see your French knitting come out at the bottom!

73

Pin Cushion

You will need:
Two discs of cloth 5"
diameter
Scraps of cloth for stuffing
Scraps of coloured felt
Two buttons for eyes
2" piece of cloth tape
Scissors, needle and thread
Wool

Paper Earrings

You will need:
Two discs of stiff coloured
paper 2" diameter
Two strips of paper 2" x 1"
Glue
Pencil, scissors, needle and
thread

Pin Cushion

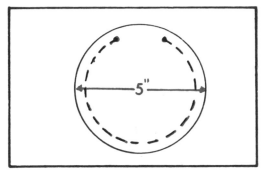

1. Sew cloth discs together with the best side inwards. Leave space at top. Turn inside out.

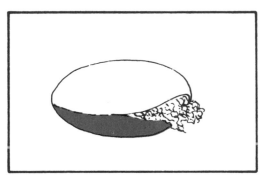

2. Stuff with scraps of cloth. Then sew together at top.

3. Sew tapes onto cushion to make a loop. Sew on piece of coloured felt, and buttons for eyes and mouth. Add wool for hair.

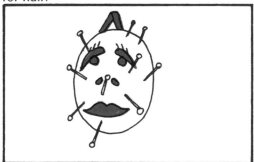

4. Now your cushion is ready to be stuck full of pins and needles!

Paper Earrings

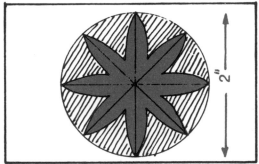

1. Draw and cut out pattern as shown from discs of coloured paper. Curl up ends of petals.

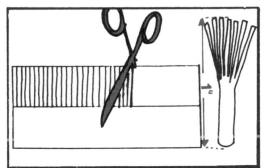

2. Make ½" cuts right along the 2" strips of paper. Roll the strips and glue edges. Push strands outwards.

3. Make a hole in the centre of each flower large enough to fit the rolled strips.

4. Push strips through centres of flowers. Push needle and thread through back and tie as shown to make loops to fit over ears.

Soft Toy

You will need:
Two discs of felt 10″
diameter
Scraps of different coloured
felt
Scraps of cloth for stuffing
Coloured wool
Scissors, needle and thread

Melon-Seed Necklace

You will need:
Dozens of dried melon seeds
Strong thread 24″ long
Needle

Soft Toy

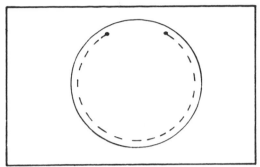

1. Sew 2 felt circles together, leaving 6″ gap to put in stuffing. Turn inside out to hide stitching.

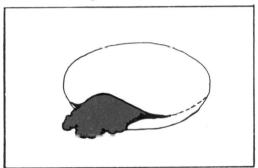

2. Stuff the body with scraps of cloth, and finish sewing the circles together.

3. Cut out patterns from coloured felt for face, arms and feet. Sew them onto body.

4. Sew on loops of coloured wool and cut ends to make hair.

Melon-Seed Necklace

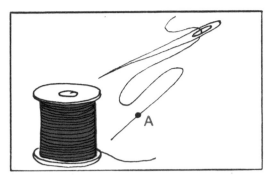

1. Knot one end of thread at A. 2″ from end. Put other end of thread through needle.

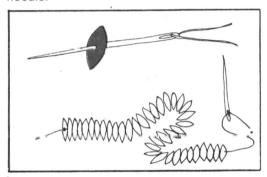

2. Push needle through middle of seed. Add more seeds until only 2″ of thread is left.

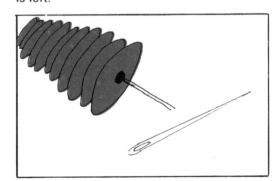

3. Take the needle off the thread, and knot the end as close as possible to the last seed.

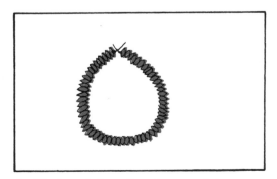

4. Tie 2 ends together to complete your necklace.

Book Cover

You will need:
Large sheet of coloured paper
Piece of white paper 3½" x 4"
Old magazines
Glue and Sellotape
Pencil, scissors, ruler

Construction Cards

You will need:
Piece of thick card 9" x 12"
Pencil and ruler
Good penknife or scissors
Coloured paints

Book Cover

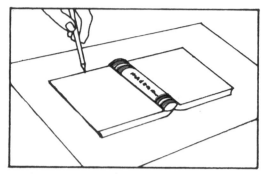

1. Open the book you wish to cover and place on coloured paper. Draw around it as shown.

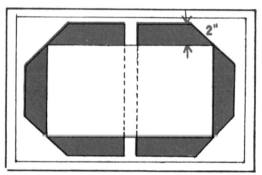

2. Add 2″ tabs to edges of outline and cut finished pattern from sheet of paper.

3. Glue paper 3½″ × 4″ on front for title. Cut out magazine pictures and glue them to cover for decoration.

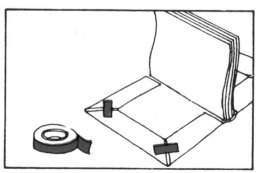

4. Turn cover over and position book as shown. Fold tabs down and tape across corners.

Construction Cards

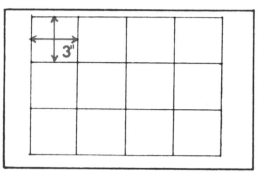

1. Draw and cut 12 squares from card 9″ × 12″.

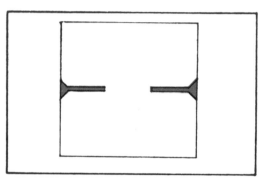

2. Cut 2 slots in each square at opposite edges 1″ deep. Angle the corners of the slots.

3. Paint each card a different colour.

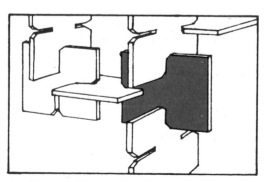

4. Now slot them together and see what you can build. Make more squares for bigger constructions.

Cotton Wool Snowman

You will need:
Piece of thin coloured card
5" x 9"
Piece of black paper 3"
square
White cotton wool
Glue, pencil
Scissors

Cotton Wool Chick

You will need:
Piece of coloured card
5" x 6"
Piece of orange card 2"
square
Yellow cotton wool
Glue, pencil
Scissors

Cotton Wool Snowman

Cotton Wool Chick

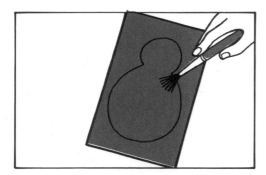

1. Draw shape of snowman on 5" x 9" card and glue this area.

1. Draw shape of chick on 5" x 6" paper and glue this area.

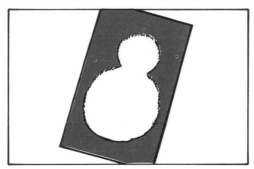

2. Press on small piece of cotton wool for head and large piece for body.

2. Press on small piece of cotton wool for head and large piece for body.

3. Draw and cut out shapes for hat, pipe, buttons and eyes from black paper.

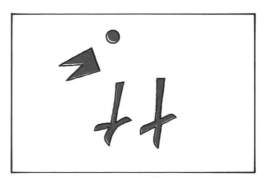

3. Draw and cut out shapes for legs, eyes and beak from orange card.

4. Glue shapes in position to complete snowman.

4. Glue shapes in position to complete chick.

Chocolate Sweetflakes

You will need:
1 oz of cornflakes (approx seven tablespoons)
½ lb of plain chocolate
Saucepan
Metal tablespoon
Large plate

Fruit Salad

You will need:
(for four people)
Two pears
Twelve grapes
Six cherries
Two oranges
Two bananas
½ pint water
4 oz sugar
Good small kitchen knife
Bowl, small saucepan

Chocolate Sweetflakes

1. Put the chocolate into the saucepan. Ask mummy to turn on the cooker ring and leave it on low.

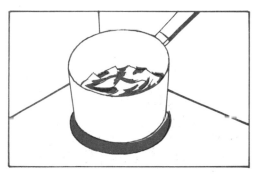

2. Place the saucepan on the ring and allow chocolate to melt. Then remove from ring and allow to cool slightly.

3. Add cornflakes and stir in with spoon until they are all coated with the chocolate.

4. Spoon into small piles on the plate and leave to set.

Fruit Salad

1. Peel the fruit and remove all the pips and cores.

2. Slice into small pieces and place in the bowl.

3. Place the water and sugar into saucepan. Ask mummy to turn on the cooker ring and leave it on high.

4. Bring to the boil and boil for three minutes. Then ask mummy to pour over fruit and leave to cool.

Apple Cat

You will need:
One large apple
One small apple
Two flat lolly sticks
Two drawing pins
Eight used matches

Potato Hedgehog

You will need:
One large potato
One small potato
Two drawing pins
Enough used matches to
cover both potatoes

Apple Cat

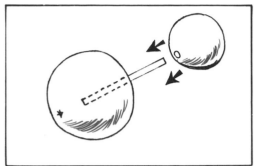

1. Push match halfway into large apple as shown. Then make small hole in small apple and fit onto match.

2. Cut lolly sticks in half and push into apples to make front paws and ears.

3. Add drawing pins for eyes.

4. Add remaining match-sticks for whiskers and tail.

Potato Hedgehog

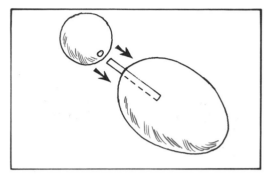

1. Push a match into large potato. Make small hole in small potato and fit onto match as shown.

2. Add drawing pins for eyes and four matches for legs.

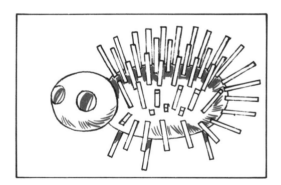

3. Push matches into body for spines.

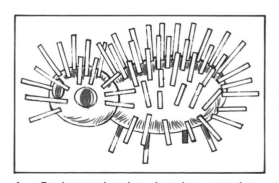

4. Push matches into head to complete.

Pressed Flowers
Pictures

You will need:
Piece of card size as
required
Flowers and leaves
Old newspapers
Heavy books
Glue

Pressed Flower
Greeting Card

You will need:
Piece of coloured paper
11" x 13"
Piece of "Cellophane" paper
4" x 5"
Flowers and leaves
Old newspapers
Heavy book
Glue, scissors
Ruler, coloured pencil

Note: Avoid using bulky flower heads as they will not press properly

Pressed Flowers Pictures

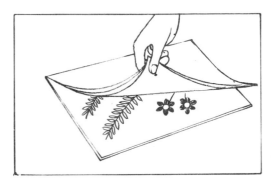

1. Carefully place flowers and leaves between several sheets of newspaper.

2. Put the newspaper in the middle of a heavy book. Place more books on top of this as extra weight and leave for 3 weeks.

3. Carefully take out the pressed flowers and glue them onto the card.

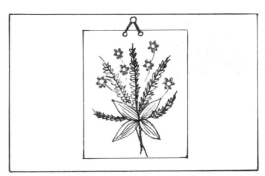

4. Try to make them look as if they are growing. Put picture in frame or punch holes in top and hang with string.

Pressed Flower Greeting Card

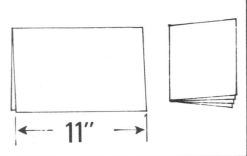

1. Fold coloured paper in half and then fold in half again. Open out flat then cut a 3" x 4" panel out of the top right segment.

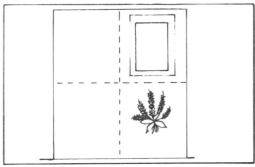

2. Glue "Cellophane" over hole. Draw 3" x 4" panel in bottom right segment. Arrange and glue pressed flowers and leaves onto the panel.

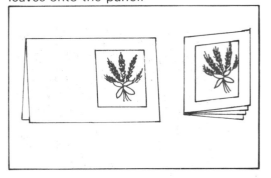

3. Fold paper so that flowers can be seen through "Cellophane" window.

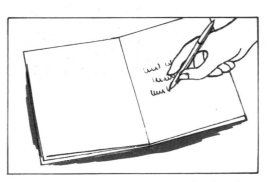

4. Write a message in the middle of your card.

DRESSING-UP
AND
PUPPETS

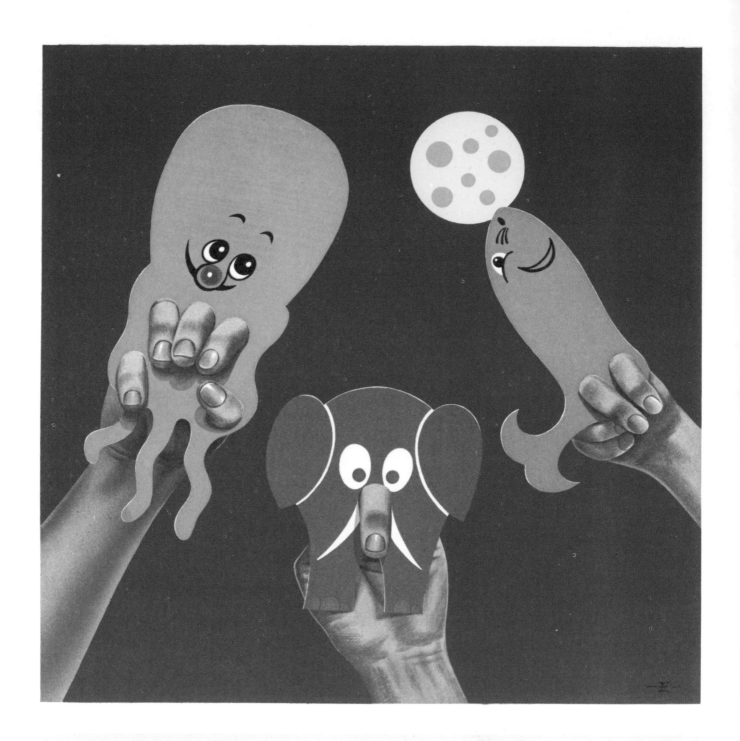

Octopus, Elephant and Seal

You will need:
Three pieces of thin cardboard
or thick paper, about
4'' x 6''

Pencil, scissors, coloured
paints

Octopus, Elephant and Seal

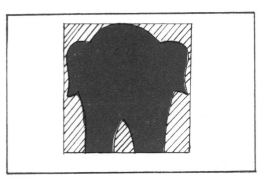

1. Draw pattern for the elephant on card or paper. Cut round the edges of the pattern.

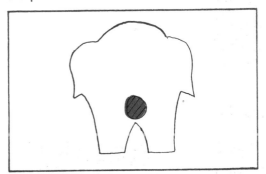

2. Cut a hole in the middle of the card large enough to put your finger through.

3. Paint on the eyes, tusks, and colour the rest of the body.

4. Put your finger through the hole from behind for the elephant's trunk.

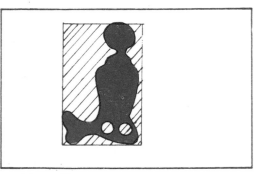

5. Draw and cut out the pattern for the seal. Make two holes at the bottom for flippers.

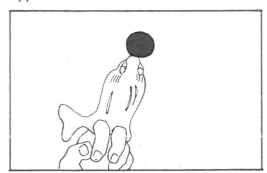

6. Decorate your seal with coloured paints, and let him perform.

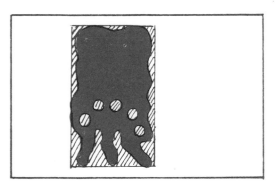

7. Draw and cut out pattern for the octopus. Make five holes at the bottom for his tentacles.

8. Decorate your octopus with coloured paints. Now he is ready to wriggle!

Silhouette Theatre

You will need:

Piece of thick cardboard
33″ × 20″
Strip of cardboard 18″ × 1½″
Strip of cardboard 18″ × 1″

Two sheets of thin cardboard
8″ × 5″
Glue
Scissors, good penknife,
coloured paints

Silhouette Theatre

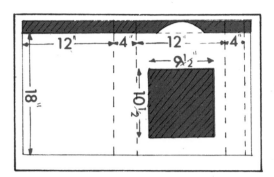

1. Draw and cut out pattern for theatre from large piece of card. Fold along dotted lines.

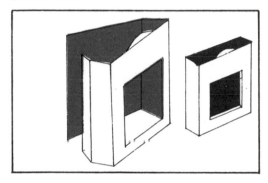

2. Glue together as shown. Paint inside black, and paint bright colours on outside.

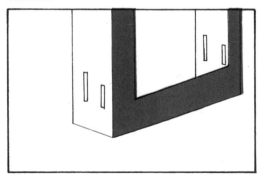

3. Cut slots at each side, as shown. 1½" slot at back, 1" slot in front.

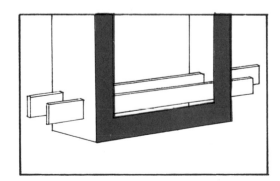

4. Paint the 18" strips of card black, and push them through the slots.

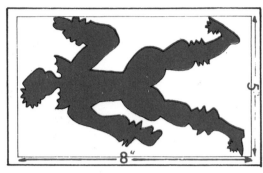

5. Draw, cut out and paint the paper clown figure as shown.

6. Draw, cut out and paint the crazy cow.

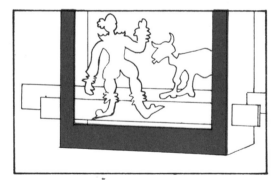

7. Glue the cow to the back strip of card, and the clown to the front.

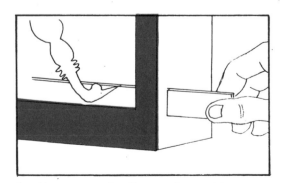

8. Now move the figures from side to side across the stage. Make other characters and put on a show.

Clown Stick Puppet

You will need:

Paper disc 2" diameter
Half-circle of thin card 12"
diameter
Round stick 18" long
Cloth 12" x 8"
Table tennis ball

Wool
Glue and Sellotape
Length of ribbon, scissors
Needle and thread,
coloured paints

Clown Stick Puppet

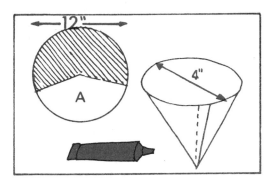

1. Cut segment A from your thin card and glue to make cone 4″ diameter.

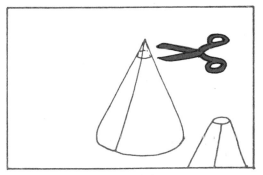

2. Cut off the point of the cone to make a hole for the stick.

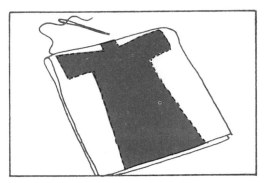

3. Fold cloth in half. Mark and stitch around shape as shown to make costume.

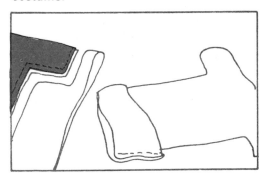

4. Cut away the cloth outside the stitches. Then turn the costume inside out.

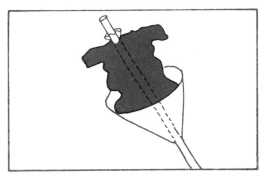

5. Cut a small hole in the top of the costume and push stick through cone and costume.

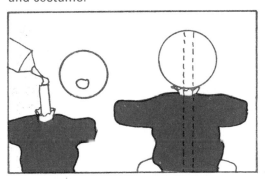

6. Make a hole in the table tennis ball. Insert the stick and glue it on as shown.

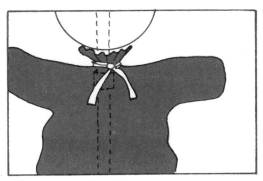

7. Wrap tape around stick as shown. Then tie costume tightly to stick just above the tape to stop it slipping.

8. Stitch bottom of costume to edge of cone. Make collar from 2″ paper disc, glue on wool for hair and paint face.

Sock-Head Clown

You will need:
An old sock
Cotton wool
Ribbon
Cloth 14″ x 7″
Wool
Scraps of cloth
Glue
Thin string
Scissors, coloured paints
Stick 5″ long
Needle and thread

Puppet Theatre

You will need:
Large carton or cardboard
box 24″ x 12″ x 19″
Two pieces of cloth
Piece of string
Scissors, needle and thread,
coloured paints or crayons

Sock-Head Clown

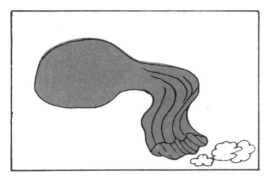

1. Stuff cotton wool into the toe of an old sock to make a head for your clown.

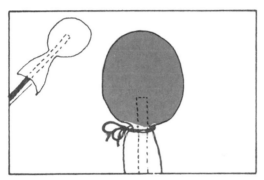

2. Push stick into centre and tie string tightly round the base of the head and make a knot.

3. Fold cloth in half and sew. Cut off excess cloth and cut hole at top. Turn inside out.

4. Tie costume to neck with ribbon. Glue on scraps of cloth to make the eyes, nose and mouth. Use wool for hair.

Puppet Theatre

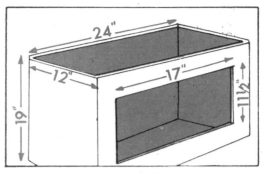

1. Cut off the top of your carton, then cut a large opening in the front, as shown

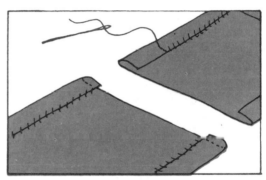

2. Cut pieces of cloth to fit opening. Fold over the top and bottom of the pieces and sew to make curtains.

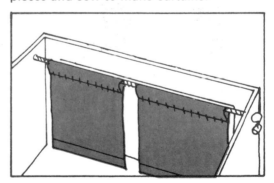

3. Make holes at the sides of the box. Thread string through the curtains. Fasten them across the stage opening.

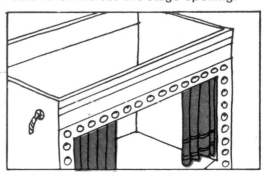

4. Cut panel out of back leaving 2″ strip across top. Open the curtains and your show can begin.

Girl Dress-Up Doll

You will need:
Piece of thick cardboard
1 ft. square

Plain paper for doll's clothes
Scissors, coloured paints

Girl Dress-Up Doll

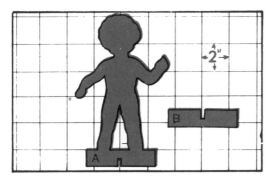

1. Draw and cut out patterns for doll and base. Fit slots together and stand her up.

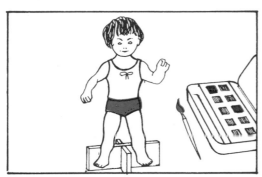

2. Paint girl's hands, legs, face and underclothes.

3. Draw and cut out pattern for coat. Decorate it. Bend tabs and place on doll's shoulders.

4. Draw and cut our pattern for dress and decorate. Dress the doll as before.

5. Draw and cut out pattern for winter sports outfit. Decorate and dress doll.

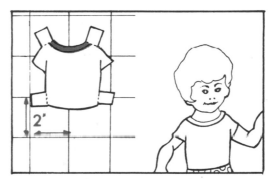

6. Draw and cut out pattern for sweater. Decorate. Place it over the dress.

7. Draw and cut out pattern for party dress. Decorate. Place over as before.

8. Draw and cut out patterns for skirt and shoes. Decorate. Bend tabs around waist and ankles.

Witch

You will need:
Large sheets of stiff black
paper
Thick card 18″ x 18″
Black crepe paper
String
Strips of brown paper 12″
long
Piece of wood 36″ long
Two pieces of cloth tape 12″
long
Pencil, scissors, Sellotape

Rabbit

You will need:
Thin card 22″ x 5″
Thin card 27″ x 18″
Two discs of thin card 10″
diameter
Paper sack or large sheet
of brown paper
Stiff paper 12″ square for tail
Glue, Sellotape
Scissors, pencil, coloured
paints

Rabbit

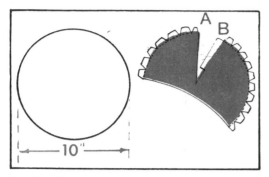

1. Cut the pattern shown from the two 10″ card discs. Glue tab B to point A.

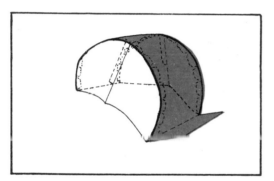

2. Bend disc tab inwards and glue to thin card 22″ × 5″ to form the cap. Fold back a flap at top edge of cap.

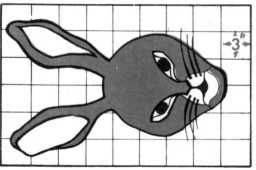

3. Draw and cut pattern for the face from card 27″ × 18″. Cut holes for eyes. Use paints or coloured paper to decorate.

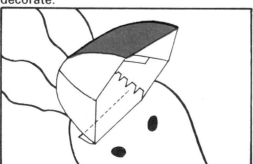

4. Glue cap to face, be sure you can see through eye holes. Cut and decorate sack or paper for body. Add tail.

Witch

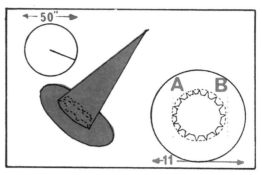

1. Make rim 11″ in diameter. Cut hole with tabs AB to fit your head. Make cone and glue to tabs on rim.

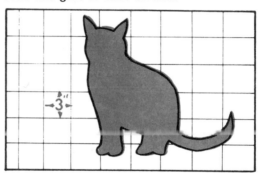

2. Draw and cut pattern for cat from thick card. Tape loop of string at back to carry it.

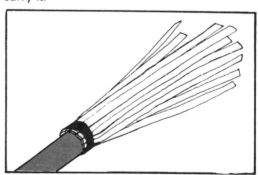

3. Tape the strips of brown paper to the piece of wood at one end to make a broom.

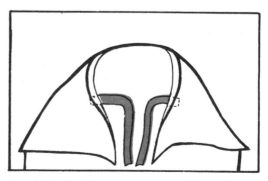

4. Cut 3 ft. of crepe paper and attach two cloth tapes to make cape.

Fairy

You will need:
White crepe paper 24″ x 20″
Thin card 24″ x 3″
Four pieces of thin card 3″
square
Thin card 28″ x 20″
Very thick card 14″ x 4″
30″ length of cloth tape
Tin foil
String
Glue and Sellotape
Scissors, pencil

Queen

You will need:
Stiff card
Crepe paper
Cotton wool
Black paper
Tin foil
Two 12″ long pieces of
cloth tape
Small pieces of coloured
paper
36″ of string
Glue and Sellotape
Scissors, pencil, ruler

Fairy

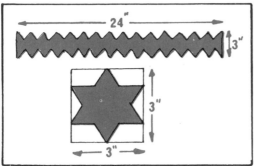

1. Draw and cut the above pattern for the crown from foilcovered card 24″ × 3″. Cut pattern for four stars from pieces of card 3″ square.

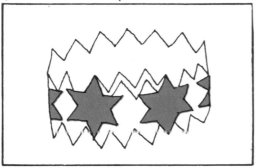

2. Glue the stars to the band to make a crown. Tape the band so that it will fit your head.

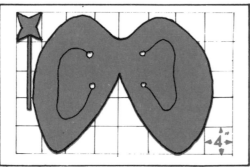

3. Draw and cut wand from foil covered card 14″ x 4″. Draw and cut wings from foil covered card 28″ x 20″. Pierce holes and attach string to fit wings.

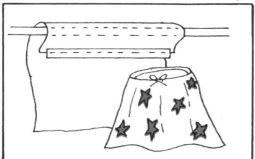

4. Lay cloth tape along 24″ edge of crepe paper, fold and tape. Decorate with foil stars. Tie around your waist for skirt.

Queen

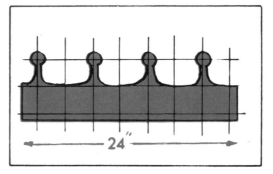

1. Cut and draw pattern as shown from the stiff card to fit your head.

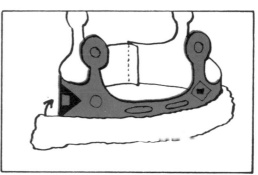

2. Glue ends together to form crown. Decorate with foil and coloured paper as shown and add cotton wool to the base.

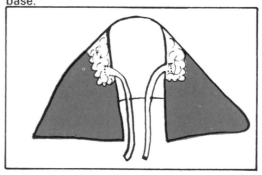

3. Tape cloth tapes to the crepe paper in the positions shown for the cape. Glue cotton wool around collar for trim.

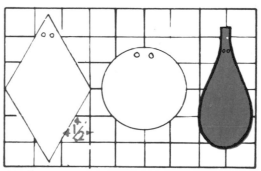

4. Glue black paper dots to cotton wool. Cut shapes from card, decorate and string together to make royal necklace.

Lion

You will need:

Thin card 22″ × 5″
Thin card 20″ × 24″
Two discs of thin card 10″
diameter
Small pieces of coloured
paper for decoration

Paper sack or large sheet of
brown paper
Stiff paper for tail
Glue and Sellotape
Scissors, pencil and
coloured paints

Lion

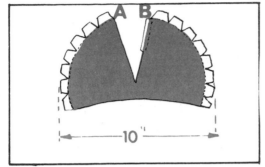

1. Cut the pattern shown from the two 10″ card discs. Glue tab B to point A.

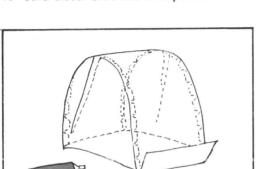

2. Bend disc tabs inwards and glue to thin card 22″ × 5″ to form the cap. Fold back a flap at top edge of cap.

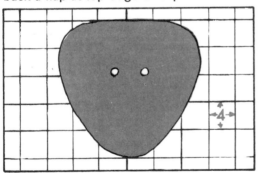

3. Draw and cut pattern for the face from card 20″ × 24″. Cut holes for eyes.

4. Decorate the lion's face by adding strips of paper for his whiskers, mane, tongue and nose.

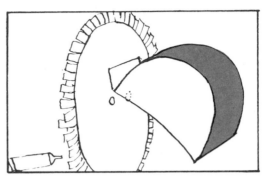

5. Glue cap to face but be sure you can see through eye holes.

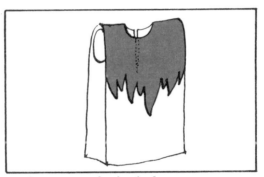

6. Cut pattern for body from paper sack or from folded sheet of brown paper. If using paper, tape sides. Decorate.

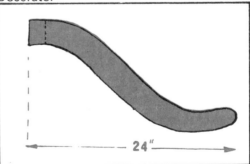

7. Draw and cut the pattern for the tail from paper. Glue it with tab to body sack as shown.

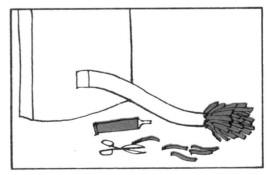

8. Cut tufts of wool and glue them to the end of the lion's tail to complete your lion.

MAKE YOUR OWN DOLL'S HOUSE

Making the House (Stage 1)

You will need:
Two cardboard boxes 18" x 12½" x 10½"
Piece of hardboard or plywood 30" x 20" for base
Scissors, glue, Sellotape, polythene bags
Pencil, penknife,
coloured paints.
(Note: Similar shape but different sized boxes can be used. In this case follow general instructions, but adjust sizes to fit your boxes)

Making the House (Stage 1)

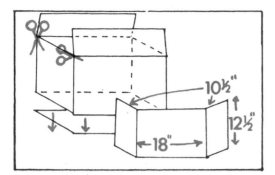

1. Cut and remove top, bottom and back of box one, leaving front and sides. Open out flat.

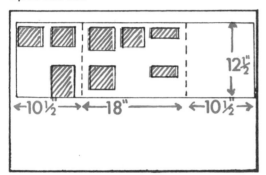

2. Draw and cut pattern above for windows. Turn over and tape pieces of polythene bags over window openings for glass.

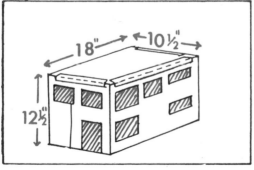

3. Cut two panels, size 10½" × 18", from front and back of box two. Fold walls and tape panels on top and bottom.

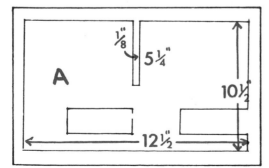

4. Make two pieces as pattern above from the sides of box two. These are for inside walls.

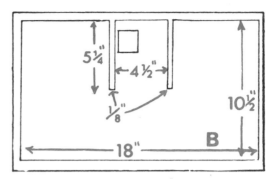

5. Draw and cut out pattern above from the back of box one. This piece divides the house into two storeys.

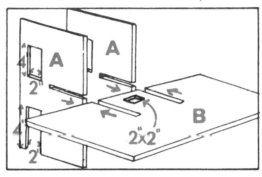

6. Paint all the walls inside and out white at this stage. Slot inside walls A into section B, as shown.

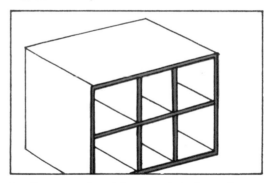

7. Tape or glue this completed section onto the inside of the house to form the rooms.

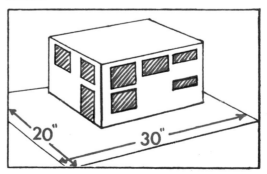

8. Glue the house onto the base in position shown. Now make roof, see separate stage.

Making the Roof (Stage 2)

You will need:

Two pieces of thick
cardboard or corrugated
board 19″ x 9½″
Two pieces of thick
cardboard or corrugated
board 7¾″ x 11½″

Two pieces of thin card
8½″ x 4½″
Two pieces of thin card
1″ x 1½″
Tape, glue, scissors,
penknife, coloured paints

Making the Roof (Stage 2)

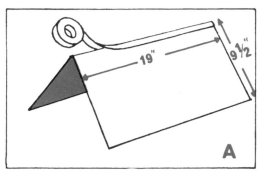

1. Take thick cards 19″ × 9½″ and join together with tape. Leave ⅛″ between to allow pieces to bend easily.

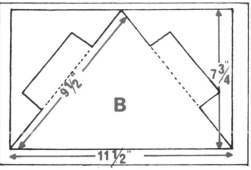

2. Draw 2 sections as above on thick card 7¾″ × 11½″. Cut and fold as shown. These are for roof supports.

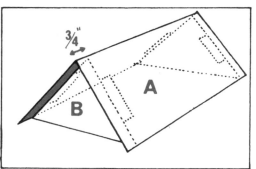

3. Glue roof supports B into roof top A. Leave ¾″ overlap at each end of roof.

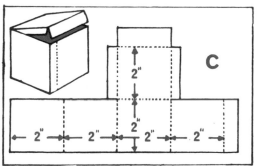

4. Draw and cut 2 sections as above from thin cards 8½″ × 4½″. Fold and glue tabs to make chimney stacks.

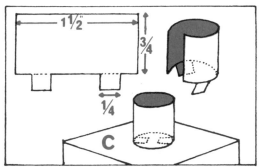

5. Draw and cut pattern for two chimney pots from thin card 1½″ × 1″. Roll and glue edge. Glue tabs onto stacks.

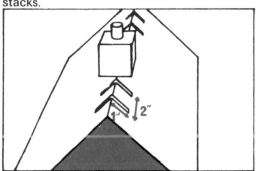

6. Cut a pair of slots 2″ apart and 1″ deep at each end of the roof top. Fit chimney stacks into slots.

7. Place the roof on the house.

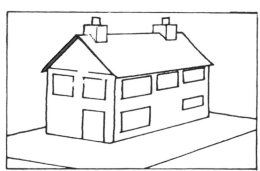

8. Decorate the roof and chimneys with coloured paints to complete the exterior of the house.

Garden Landscape (Stage 3)

You will need:

Coloured paper 4½'' square
Coloured paper for path
Thin card 8'' x 4''
Thin card 5'' x 4''
Two cotton reels

Two small twigs
Egg carton lid or paper tray
Glue, scissors, pencil, ruler
Coloured paints

Garden Landscape (Stage 3)

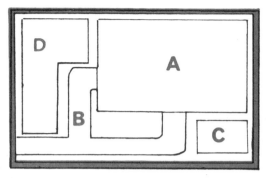

1. Draw out the plan on your base in pencil. A is the house; B path; C patio and D pool.

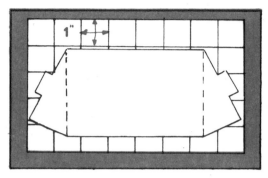

5. Draw and cut paper pattern for canopy over door. Fold and glue over door.

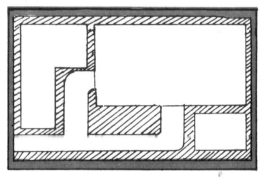

2. Paint the shaded areas green.

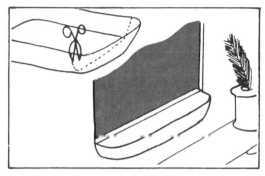

6. Cut an egg carton lid or paper tray to make window box. Glue below window.

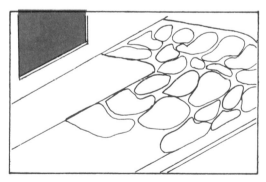

3. Cut irregular shapes in grey or brown paper and glue them to the paths.

7. Cut twenty 1" squares from 5" × 4" card. Glue them on the base to make patio (C).

4. Cut and glue on 2 pieces of coloured paper 2¼" × 4½" from paper 4½" square, for front doors. Paint on door knobs.

8. Paint 2 reels white and put them at either side of the front door, with a small twig in each.

Garden Furniture and Pool (Stage 4)

You will need:
Sheet of thin coloured card
Toilet roll tube
Cotton reel
Lolly stick
Pieces of thin card for sides
of pool: 12" x 4", 8" x 4",

7" x 4", 5" x 4" and two 4"
squares
Glue
Pencil, scissors, coloured
paints

114

Garden Furniture and Pool (Stage 4)

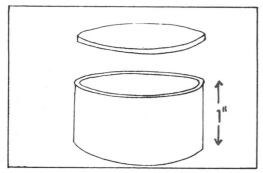

1. Cut four 1″ lengths from toilet roll tube. Cut four discs from card to fit the tops and glue into place for chairs.

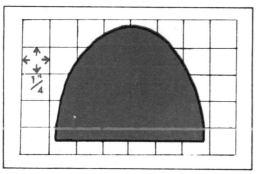

2. Draw and cut pattern for seat back from card and glue to one seat.

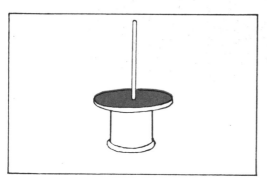

3. For the table glue a 1½″ disc of card to top of cotton reel. Push the stick through the centre.

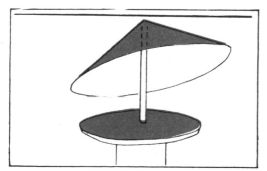

4. Make sunshade from a 4½″ disc of paper. Cut and glue into cone. Fix on top of stick as shown.

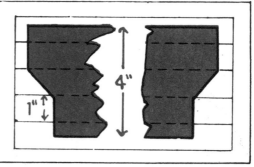

5. Draw and cut out above shapes at each end of the cards for sides of pool. Fold along dotted lines.

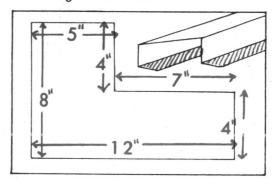

6. Glue into position around pool, following the above plan. Paint bottom of pool blue.

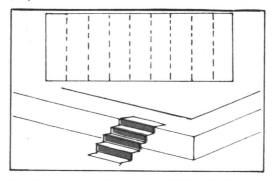

7. Make steps from card 2¼″ × 1″. Fold at every ¼″ as shown and glue into place.

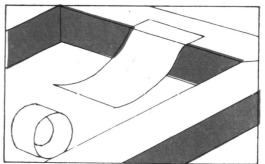

8. Cut two 2″ × 1″ strips of card. Curve one for chute and make other into tube for decoration. Glue both to pool.

Lounge Furniture (Stage 5)

You will need:

Egg box carton lid
Thin coloured card
Stiff coloured paper
Tin foil 3½" x 1½"

Scissors, glue, ruler,
coloured paints
Pencil

Lounge Furniture (Stage 5)

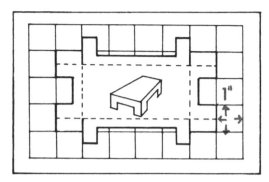

1. Draw pattern for table on card. Cut along solid lines, fold along dotted lines and glue together.

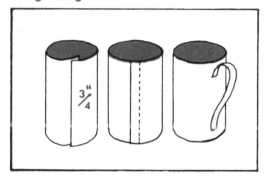

2. Cut a 1" × ¾" piece of card. Glue into a tube for jug. Stick on a thin strip of card for handle.

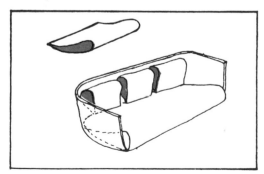

3. Cut an egg box lid as shown, to make couch.

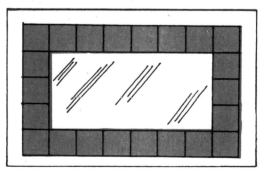

4. Cut and bend squares of paper for cushions. Glue to couch as shown. Use smaller squares for little cushions.

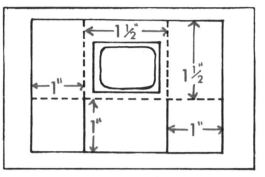

5. Draw pattern above on card for T.V. Cut along solid lines, fold along dotted lines and glue together to make box.

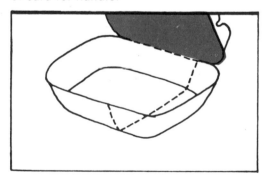

6. Draw and cut pattern for T.V. table from card. Fold along dotted lines and glue together. Decorate with paints.

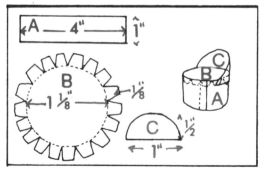

7. Draw and cut patterns for three seats from card. Roll 4" strips into tubes and glue on cushions and backs.

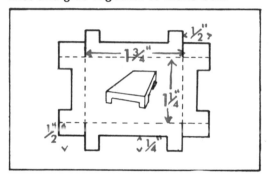

8. Cut card 4" × 2" for frame and glue a piece of foil 3½" × 1½" inside to make a mirror. Glue to wall.

Bedroom Furniture (Stage 6)

You will need:

Stiff coloured paper

Lolly stick

Thin coloured card

Pencil, scissors, ruler

Glue, coloured paints

Bedroom Furniture (Stage 6)

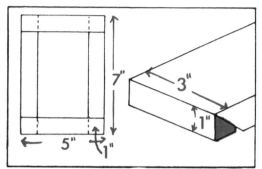

1. Draw and cut pattern for bed from card 7″ x 5″. Fold along lines and glue.

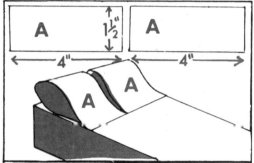

2. Fold 2 pieces of thin card 4″ × 1½″ as shown. Glue to top of bed for pillows.

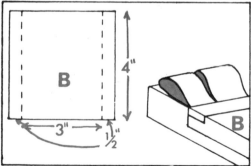

3. Fold piece of paper 4″ × 4″ as shown, and glue on bed for bedspread. Add strip of white paper for sheet.

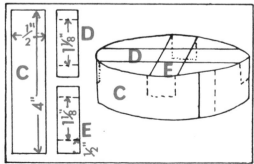

4. Draw and cut paper patterns for lampshade and glue together as shown.

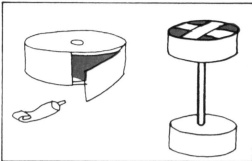

5. Make lamp base from two cardboard discs 1½″ diameter and paper strip, as shown. Push stick in base and glue shade on top.

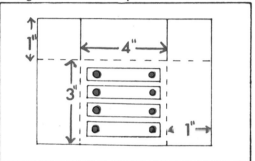

6. Draw and cut card 6″ × 4″ for chest of drawers. Fold along dotted lines and glue. Decorate with paints.

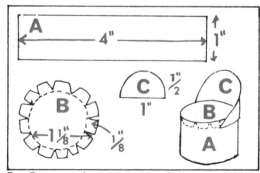

7. Draw and cut patterns for two seats from card. Roll 4″ strips into tubes and glue on cushions and backs.

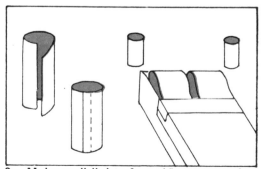

8. Make wall-lights from 1″ squares of paper. Roll into tubes and glue to wall above bed.

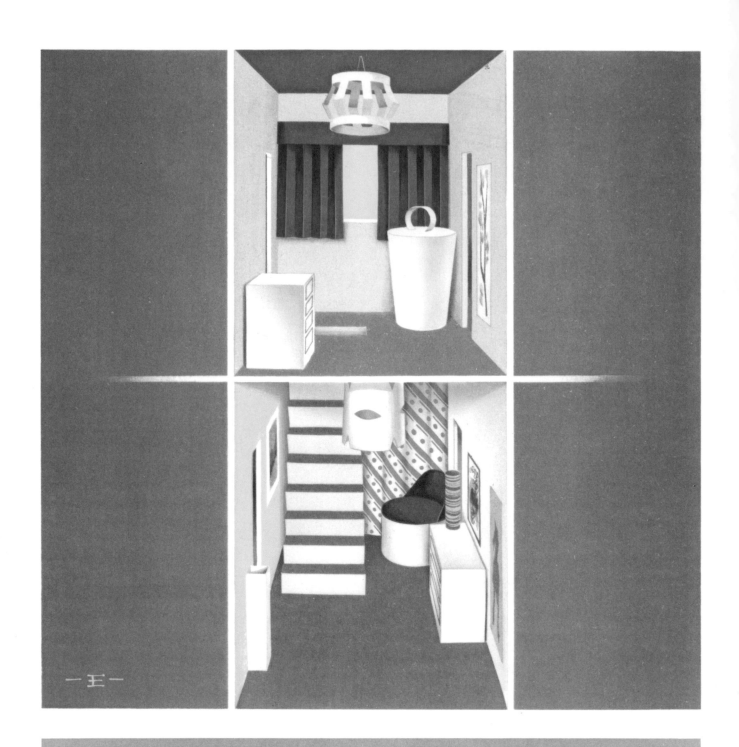

Hall and Landing Furniture (Stage 7)

You will need:

Coloured paper
Thin card

Coloured paints
Scissors, glue, pencil, ruler

Hall and Landing Furniture (Stage 7)

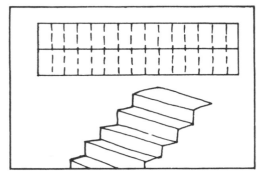

1. Make the stairs from card 10½" × 2". Fold on dotted lines as shown.

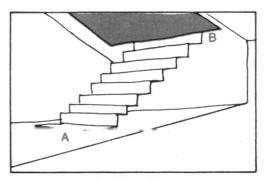

2. Glue one end of the staircase to hall floor and the other end to the opening in the landing floor.

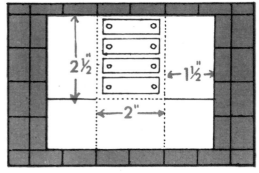

3. Draw and cut pattern for landing chest from card. Fold along dotted lines and glue together. Decorate.

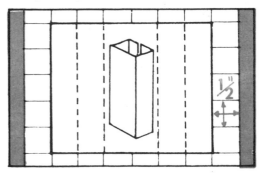

4. Draw and cut pattern for umbrella stand from card 3" × 2½". Fold on dotted lines and glue to wall in hall.

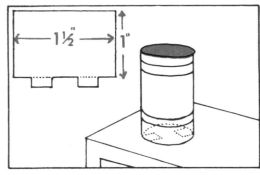

5. Draw and cut pattern for lamp on a 1¼" × 1½" piece of paper. Roll and glue as shown. Glue onto hall chest.

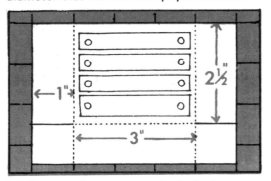

6. Draw and cut pattern for basket from card 8" × 7". Bend and glue. Glue on 2" diameter disc for lid. Add paper handle.

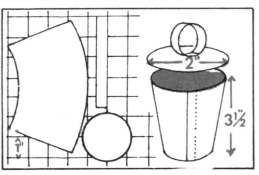

7. Draw and cut pattern for hall chest from card. Fold along dotted lines and glue together. Decorate as shown.

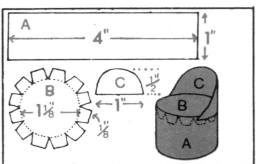

8. Draw and cut pattern for hall chair from card. Roll 4" strip into tube and glue on cushion and back.

Kitchen Furniture (Stage 8)

You will need:

Thin card

Scissors, pencil, ruler

Glue, coloured paints

Kitchen Furniture (Stage 8)

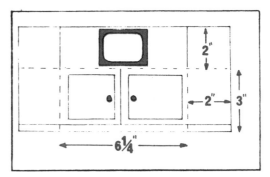

1. Draw and cut pattern above for sink unit from card. Fold along dotted lines.

2. Glue together as shown, and decorate with paints. Place in position in kitchen.

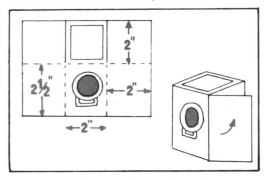

3. Draw and cut pattern above for washing machine from card. Fold along dotted lines and glue together. Decorate as shown.

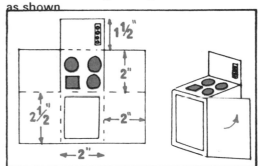

4. Draw and cut pattern for cooker from card. Fold along dotted lines and glue together. Decorate as shown.

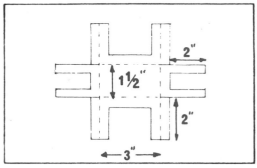

5. Draw pattern for table on card. Cut along solid lines, fold along dotted lines and glue.

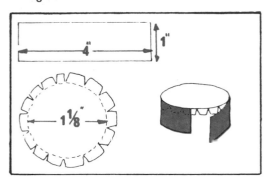

6. Draw and cut pattern for chair from card. Roll 4″ strip into tube and glue on cushion as shown.

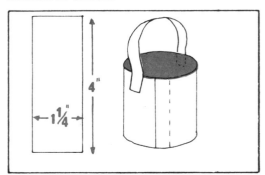

7. Draw and cut pattern for bucket from card. Roll 4″ strip into tube and glue. Add small card strip for handle.

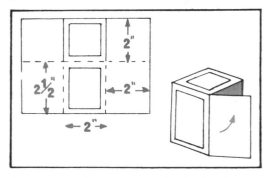

8. Draw and cut pattern for fridge from card. Fold along dotted lines and glue as shown. Decorate with paints.

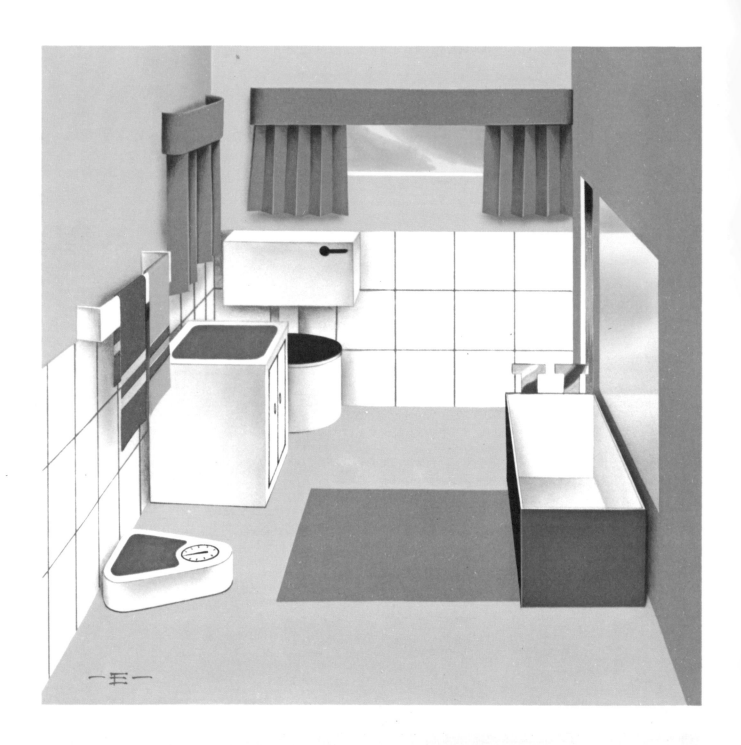

Bathroom Furniture (Stage 9)

You will need:

Thick card ¼″ x 3″

Thin card

Tin foil

Toilet roll tube

Coloured paper

Scissors, glue, ruler, pencil

Black paint

Bathroom Furniture (Stage 9)

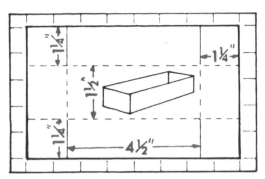

1. Draw pattern for bath on card 7″×4″. Cut along solid lines, fold along dotted lines and glue together.

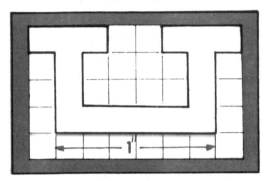

2. Glue foil onto card 1¼″×1″. Draw and cut pattern above for bath taps from it and glue into position.

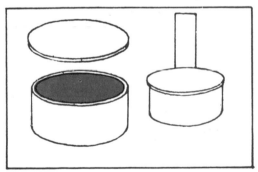

3. Cut a 1″ piece of tube for toilet. Glue a paper disc on the top. Glue ¼″×3″ thick card in position shown.

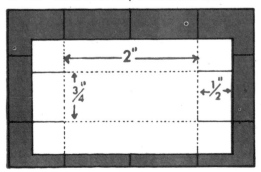

4. Draw and cut pattern for cistern from card 3″×1¾″. Fold on dotted lines and glue together. Paint on handle.

5. Fold ¼″ of toilet upright over and glue on cistern as shown.

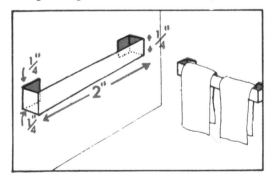

6. Draw and cut pattern for scales from card 3″×2½″. Fold along dotted lines and glue together. Decorate with paint.

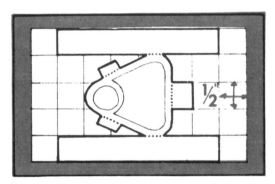

7. Cut and fold card 3″×¼″ for towel rail. Glue to wall. Cut two pieces of paper 2″×¾″, fold and hang as shown.

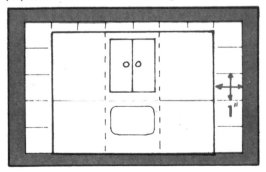

8. Draw and cut pattern for cupboard from card 6″×4½″. Fold along dotted lines and glue. Decorate as shown.

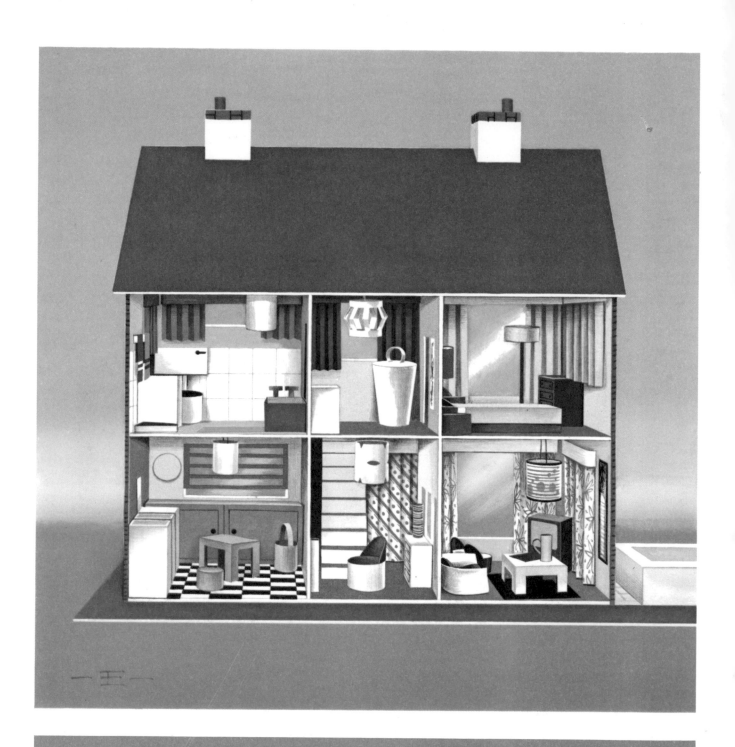

Decorating the Rooms (Stage 10)

You will need
Thin card
Scissors, glue,
needle and thread,

Sellotape
Coloured paper